# RICHARD NIXON
*American Politician*

Notable Americans

# RICHARD NIXON
## *American Politician*

**Rachel Barron**

## MORGAN REYNOLDS
## Incorporated

**Greensboro**

**RICHARD NIXON:** *American Politician*

Copyright © 1999 by Rachel Barron

Photo credits: AP/Wide World Photos; National Archives; The Richard Nixon Library &
Birthplace.

Library of Congress Cataloging-in-Publication Data
Barron, Rachel.
  Richard Nixon: American politician / Rachel Barron. —1st ed.
      p.  cm. — (Notable Americans)
  Includes bibliographical references and index.
  ISBN  1-883846-33-1
      1. Nixon, Richard M. (Richard Milhous), 1913-1994—Juvenile literature.
2. Presidents—United States—Biography—Juvenile literature.  I. Title  II. Series.
E856.B37  1998
973.924' 092—dc21
[b]

                                                              98-29836
                                                                  CIP
                                                                   AC

Printed in the United States of America
First Edition

## *Dedication*

*For my parents, who encouraged me to write,
and my husband, my greatest supporter.*

# Contents

Richard Milhous Nixon

# Chapter One

## The Last Press Conference

It was the morning after Election Day 1962, and Richard Milhous Nixon, the Republican candidate for governor of California, had been up most of the night. He had spent hours, alone, in front of the television in his room in the Beverly Hilton Hotel, brooding over the results of the election. Before going to bed, he had telegraphed his Democratic opponent, the incumbent governor Pat Brown, and congratulated him on his victory. Brown had won by nearly 300,000 votes.

But conceding defeat to Brown had not been easy. Nixon hated to lose. Only two years before, after serving as vice president for eight years, he had run for president of the United States and suffered an agonizing defeat. Massachusetts senator John Kennedy had won the presidency in one of the closest elections in history. The 1960 presidential campaign had exhausted him and his wife, Pat, who was tired of the grueling campaign trips, the speeches, the handshaking. Pat had resisted the idea of Nixon running for governor of California. At first, Nixon himself did not want to make the effort, but he had been talked into running by some of his friends in the Republican Party. These were many of the same people who had arranged for him to first enter politics back in 1946, and Nixon did not think it was wise to disappoint them.

Now, the morning after this humiliating defeat, a roomful of reporters waited for Nixon to make a statement. It was customary for the losing candidate to make a final appearance before the media. Nixon, however, had decided he was not up to facing them. He did not like reporters. He felt many of them were not fair to him, that they were more critical of him than of his opponents. His press secretary, Herb Klein, said he would go to the press conference instead.

Nixon gathered together his campaign staff and thanked them for all they had done. Some of the secretaries cried. A tearful assistant hugged him. There was nothing left to do but leave the hotel and return home.

A few minutes later, as Nixon rode the elevator down to the lobby, he had a change of heart. He would go to the press conference after all. The reporters were surprised to see Nixon step to the microphone. He had no remarks prepared, so he spoke off the cuff. "Now that Mr. Klein has made a statement, now that all the members of the press are so delighted that I lost, I would just like to make a statement of my own," he began.

Nixon seemed calm as he congratulated Governor Brown on his victory. Then, suddenly, he shook his fist at the reporters. "As I leave you I want you to know—just think how much you're going to be missing. You won't have Nixon to kick around anymore, because, gentlemen, this is my last press conference, and it will be one in which I have welcomed the opportunity to test wits with you."

He waved awkwardly and left the room. The stunned reporters stared at each other. Nixon was such a fighter. No one ever expected him to quit politics, certainly not in an emotional outburst like this.

Years later, Nixon admitted: "To the great majority of my supporters and virtually all of the press, my so-called last press conference was a personal and political disaster." The California newspapers ridiculed Nixon. The ABC television network aired a thirty-minute television show called "The Political Obituary of Richard Nixon."

Evangelist Billy Graham wrote Nixon a letter, urging him to apologize to the press and to not give up on politics. He need not have worried. Nixon never apologized, but even in the car on the way home from his "last press conference," he was plotting his comeback.

At the time, few people thought Nixon's career could be revived after such an embarrassment. Yet, just six years later, Richard Nixon would be elected president of the United States. And, just six years after that, he would be the first president forced to resign from office.

# Chapter Two

## The Early Years

In the early years of the twentieth century, in a little town called Yorba Linda, California, on the edge of a desert with dusty winds and little rainfall, Frank and Hannah Nixon were pursuing the American dream. They had a small farm where they grew lemons. It was a tough life with little profit to show for their efforts. Most of the people who lived in Yorba Linda were, like the Nixons, Quakers. The Quakers did not believe in drinking or dancing. They did believe in hard work and sacrifice. Church activities were the main source of recreation.

Hannah, a quiet woman who had been raised in a devout Quaker family, fit right in. Hannah used what the Quakers called "plain speech." Instead of "you," they said "thee." Frank, a boisterous man of Irish descent who had converted to the Quaker faith after marrying Hannah, was sometimes too loud for his fellow church members. He loved to argue, and one of his favorite topics was politics. In 1909, the Nixons had their first child, a son they named Harold.

Times were hard on the lemon grove. Frank had one shirt, one pair of pants, and one suit for church. On some nights, they had nothing to eat but corn meal. Hannah worked in the field and cared for Harold.

On January 9, 1913, Hannah delivered her second son. She named him Richard Milhous Nixon, after Richard the Lion-Hearted, king of England. "Milhous" had been her maiden name. The baby was a large one—eleven pounds—and he had a loud, screaming cry. When Richard was two years old, Hannah had a third son, Donald.

Fortunately for his parents, Richard grew from a fussy infant into a quiet and smart little boy. He was rather serious, though, and didn't smile a lot. In 1918, when Richard was five, his mother was pregnant again. One day, his father told the three boys that they were about to get a new, real live doll. Years later, in a college essay, Richard wrote: "Naturally we then began to quarrel over whose doll it would be, although each of us wished to have it merely to keep the others from getting it." Nine-year-old Harold told his younger brothers that the "doll" was actually a baby, but he swore them to secrecy. Richard wrote in his college essay that when he finally saw the baby, whom his parents named Arthur, he was disappointed to see that he was not as pretty as a store bought doll.

The Nixons were strict disciplinarians. Frank would whip his sons with a strap for misbehaving. One of his rules was that they could not play near the canal that ran by their house. The banks were slippery, and some children had drowned. One day Frank caught Harold and Richard swimming in the canal. He hauled them out, then flung them back in, yelling, "Do you like water? Have some more of it!"

Despite Frank's temper, the boys dreaded Hannah's discipline more. In a 1968 campaign film, Richard said that his mother's tongue "was never sharp, but she would just sit you down and she would talk very quietly and then when you got through you had been through an emotional experience. In our family, we would always prefer spanking." Those who knew Hannah described her as a saintly, hard-working woman. She was a fine mother, but not affectionate.

Hannah dealt with Frank's temper by keeping quiet and not crossing him when he was angry, and Richard learned to do the same. When Donald and Harold were arguing with their father, Richard would be off by himself, reading a book. By age six, he was reading the newspapers and discussing current events with Frank.

By age eleven, Richard already had great dreams for his life. When he heard his father talking about the corrupt politicians who had accepted bribes in the Teapot Dome scandal of 1924, he avidly read the papers to find out more. "When I get big," he said, "I'll be a lawyer they can't bribe."

Frank Nixon eventually grew tired of scraping for a living on the lemon farm. He sold it and moved the family to nearby Whittier, another Quaker town. Frank went to work in the oil fields, but two years later he decided the only way to truly prosper was to own his own business. He opened a grocery store, the Nixon Market. The entire family worked to make the store a success. Hannah baked pies that became a popular item with the customers, and the boys helped out when they were not in school.

Although he stayed out of arguments at home, Richard showed a real interest in debating while he was still in grammar school. Another of his talents was playing the piano. His parents thought his musical talent was worth encouraging and sent him to live with an aunt for six months so that she could give him daily piano lessons. He also took violin lessons from another teacher. In the end, though, he decided he did not like music enough to make it his career and returned to his family.

Many years later, he told about his homecoming, and his description revealed something interesting about the Nixon family: "Like any twelve-year-old, I was happy to see them after what seemed like a very long time. As soon as he saw me alone, my youngest brother, Arthur, greeted me with a solemn kiss on the cheek. I later learned that he had asked my mother if it would be proper for him to kiss me since I had been away. Even at that early age he had acquired our family's reticence about open displays of affection."

Just a few months later, Arthur became ill. At first the family thought it was a mild sickness, but his condition worsened until all he wanted to do was to rest and sleep; he even lost interest in eating. Several doctors came to the house, but none could say exactly what was wrong with Arthur. In recalling his illness years later, Richard said one day Arthur "called my mother into the room. He put his arms around her and said that he wanted to pray before he went to sleep. Then, with closed eyes, he repeated that age-old child's prayer which ends with those simple yet beautiful words: 'If I should die before I awake, I pray Thee, Lord, my soul to take...'"

Arthur's death changed Richard's life. Hannah Nixon said that, after Arthur's death, Richard seemed to want to succeed even more, as if he were trying to make up for the loss of Arthur.

There were other tragedies in store for the Nixon family. Older brother Harold, who had grown into a handsome, popular, fun-loving young man, had already begun what would be a long battle with tuberculosis, an infectious disease of the lungs. In those days, tuberculosis was usually incurable. To try to recover, many victims went to drier climates to stay in sanitariums, which were sort of like resorts for sick people. Hannah took Harold to Prescott, Arizona, known for its high, dry mountains. But she found that she could not afford to put Harold in any of the expensive sanitariums. Instead, she rented a cabin for $25 a month and took in three other tuberculosis patients to pay her expenses. Hannah did all the cooking and cleaning.

Four hundred miles away, at home in Whittier, Richard was now in high school and was in charge of the vegetable counter at the Nixon Market. He got up every morning at 4 a.m. to drive the pickup truck to Los Angeles, where he bought vegetables, then drove back to the store and set them out on the counter before going to school.

When he was younger, Richard had always been a loner, but in high school he joined the Latin club, the debate club, the school newspaper, the orchestra, and the football team. He also acted in a few plays. He threw his 140-pound body into football with all his might. He enjoyed playing the sport, but he was not very good and took quite a beating. Although he was well known, Richard had few close friends. He was not a kid who relaxed, told jokes, and made small talk. He ran for student body president but lost.

Richard's grades were excellent and he hoped to go to college in the East. He won a scholarship to Harvard University and was in contention for one from Yale University. But Harold's illness had drained the family's money, and although the scholarship would have paid his tuition, his room and board and the cost of traveling from California to the East Coast were too much for the family to afford. Richard ended up going to nearby Whittier College, a Quaker college of about 400 students. His high school girlfriend, Ola Florence Welsh, went there, too.

Although Richard was seventeen, a year younger than most of his classmates, he was elected president of the freshman class. Whittier had

Richard Nixon (standing on the wagon wheel) was born in this house in Yorba Linda, California on January 9, 1913. Notice the bridge crossing the irrigation canal that the Nixon sons were not allowed to play near.

no fraternities, but it did have one men's society called the Franklins. Richard and his friends viewed the Franklins as rich and stuffy. They wore tuxedoes to all their social events and even had their group photo made in formal attire.

Richard organized a new group, called the Orthogonians, made up mostly of football players and young men from more modest families, many of whom were working their way through college. The group had its picture made in open-collar shirts as a deliberate contrast to the Franklins. Richard wrote the charter and made up a symbol, motto, and song for the group. The group's first project was a dance in the school gym. Richard had to ask the college president's permission because the Quakers frowned on dancing. Richard took Ola Florence to the dance, even though he actually hated dancing and was very awkward at it.

During school breaks, Richard, Donald, and their father drove the fourteen-hour, 400-mile trip across the desert to Arizona to see their mother and Harold. They spent part of two summers there. In Arizona, Richard took odd jobs, such as working as a janitor at a swimming pool or plucking chickens. "It was during Harold's long illness that my mother showed the depth of her character and faith," Richard later wrote. "In addition to the wrenching physical and emotional strain of nursing, the very fact of separation from the rest of us was very hard on my mother." It is evident that the strain affected the entire Nixon family.

After three years in Prescott, Harold was no better, and he missed his home terribly. It was decided he should come back to Whittier. Harold was not a good patient. He refused to stay in bed as the doctors had ordered. One day, he said he would like to go across the San Bernardino Mountains to see the desert. Frank Nixon dropped everything and rented a wooden house trailer. The rest of the family saw Harold and Frank off one morning, expecting them to be gone about a month. They returned only three days later. Harold had become sicker. Later, in his memoirs, Richard wrote: "I can still remember his voice when he described the beauty of the wild flowers in the foothills and the striking sight of snow in the mountains. I sensed that he knew this was the last time he would ever see them."

Not long after that, Harold asked Richard to drive him downtown.

This picture of the Nixon store was taken in the 1940s. Richard had to stock the produce section every morning before going to school.

He wanted to buy an electric cake mixer for their mother's birthday. "He barely had the strength to walk with me into the hardware store. We had them wrap the mixer as a birthday present, and we hid it at home at the top of a closet.

"The next morning he said that we should postpone giving our presents to mother until that night because he did not feel well and wanted to rest. About three hours later I was studying in the college library when I received a message to come home. When I got there, I saw a hearse parking in front of the house. My parents were crying uncontrollably as the undertaker carried out Harold's body. My mother said that right after I left for school Harold asked her to put her arms around him and hold him very close. He had never been particularly religious, but he looked at her and said, 'This is the last time I will see you, until we meet in heaven.' He died an hour later. That night I got the cake mixer out and gave it to my mother and told her that it was Harold's gift to her."

After Harold's death, his mother said in an interview years later, Richard "sank into a deep, impenetrable silence. From that time on, it seemed that Richard was trying to be *three* sons in one, striving even harder than before to make up to his father and me for our loss."

Richard kept up good grades at Whittier College even though he continued working at the store, acting and debating. He was a loyal member of the football team, although he mostly warmed the bench. The coach, Wallace "Chief" Newman, became a mentor and second father to him. Newman was an American Indian who was "tall and ramrod-straight," Nixon wrote. "He inspired in us the idea that if we worked hard enough and played hard enough, we could beat anybody. He believed in always playing cleanly, but he also believed that there is a great difference between winning and losing. He used to say, 'Show me a good loser, and I'll show you a loser.'" That philosophy would have a profound influence on Richard's life.

Richard's popularity on campus was evident when the campus newspaper did a story about him during his junior year. It was accompanied by what would be the first of thousands of cartoons of him published over his lifetime. It showed the dark, bushy hair, the thick

The Nixon family in Yorba Linda. The children are (from left): Harold, Donald, and Richard.

eyebrows, the bulging jowls, and the "ski-jump" nose.

Richard and Ola Florence continued to date throughout their four years of college, although they often disagreed. At one dance they had an argument and Richard drove off and left Ola there; she had to call her mother for a ride. Ola was the most popular girl on campus, and Richard, though well known, was still socially awkward. He had no close friends of his own. Everyone assumed they would get married, but by the time they graduated from Whittier, their relationship was on its last legs. In any case, Richard was too ambitious to do what most young people did right after college—get married and have children. He saw a promising announcement on a bulletin board of $250 tuition scholarships to the new law school at Duke University in Durham, North Carolina. He applied and was overjoyed when he learned that he had received one.

Richard began law school all the way across the continent the next fall. He had never been so far away from home. He had also never experienced such a demanding academic environment. Duke was much tougher and more competitive than little Whittier College. Richard threw himself into his studies, spending long hours in the library and staying up far into the night, even on Saturdays. Although he and Ola had broken up, he continued to write her long, sad letters about how homesick and discouraged he felt. He never dated anyone during his time at Duke.

He still had very little money. A maintenance man for the university discovered Richard living in an abandoned tool shed in the woods near campus. The maintenance man exclaimed that Richard would freeze to death. "I'll manage all right if you don't run me out," Richard replied. The maintenance man, deciding that this young man must have wanted an education very badly, decided not to report him.

Nixon rented a couple of other cheap rooms and inexpensive apartments during his time at Duke. It was so cold in one apartment that he took all of his showers at the university gym and kept his shaving kit hidden behind books in the library. He started each day at five a.m., studying until classes began, then worked in the library in the afternoon

Richard dated Ola Florence Welsh for most of his teenage years.

for thirty-five cents an hour, then studied in the evening until at least midnight.

Late in the spring of his junior year, he won the race for president of the Duke Student Bar Association. The time it took to run for the office took away from his studies and his grades slipped. He became particularly worried about his class rank. One day, Richard and a couple of his friends passed by the dean's office. The grades and class standings were late in being posted, and the three young students noticed that there was an opening near the top of the dean's office door. Since Richard was the thinnest, they hoisted him up through the opening, and he climbed down into the office and opened the door for his friends. They managed to find the key to the dean's desk and to open it and look in the drawers. They only looked at the grades and did not change any, but years later critics pointed to this incident as an early sign of Richard Nixon's corrupt nature. His friends, however, said it was nothing but a harmless prank.

During Christmas break of his final year of law school, Nixon made the rounds of all the top law firms in New York City, hoping to get a position. The two students who ranked first and second in the class received job offers, but Richard, ranked third, did not. He returned home to Whittier, where he had little trouble finding a place there in the firm of Wingert and Bewley. One of the partners, Thomas Bewley, took Nixon under his wing.

The work at Wingert and Bewley was not exciting. Nixon mainly handled divorce, traffic, and drunk-driving cases. Nevertheless, he worked very hard—sometimes sixteen hours a day—and earned the respect of his fellow lawyers. Bewley, who was the city attorney, named Nixon the assistant city attorney and entrusted him with most of the city's legal work.

Nixon had always enjoyed acting and became involved in the local theater. At an audition he spotted Pat Ryan, a young schoolteacher. Nixon could not take his eyes off her the entire evening. She was a tall, slender, pretty redhead who moved very gracefully. It seemed that everyone there wanted to talk to her.

When the audition was over, Nixon offered Pat and her girlfriend a ride home. Much to his disappointment, the friend sat in the middle, between him and Pat. Nixon leaned over and said, "I'd like to have a date with you." Pat just laughed and said, "I'm too busy."

After the theater group's next meeting, Nixon again drove the two women home, and again Pat turned down his request for a date. The third night he drove them home, he leaned across the seat and asked, yet again, "When are you going to give me that date?" Pat just laughed and shook her head. Nixon pointed his finger at her. "Don't laugh," he said. "Someday I'm going to marry you." Pat just laughed harder than ever.

Pat had been born Thelma Catherine Ryan on March 16, 1912, in Ely, Nevada. When she was fourteen, her mother died of stomach cancer. After that, Pat rose at dawn to make breakfast for her father and two brothers before going to school. She returned in the evening to do the cooking, sewing, laundry, and cleaning.

When it was time for Thelma to go to college, her father was taken ill with tuberculosis. She went to a junior college as a part-time student and got a job in a bank so that she could take care of him. When he died, she decided to legally change her name to Pat, the nickname he had given her because she was born so close to St. Patrick's Day.

Pat finally agreed to date Nixon, but she continued to go out with others, too. Nixon, willing to do anything to be with her, even drove her to meet other young men so she would not have to take the trolley. He would drop her off, then hang around in a movie theater or hotel lobby until it was time to pick her up. Nixon had learned from his experience with Ola that he would have to do things with Pat's friends and participate in activities that she enjoyed. One of them was ice-skating. Although he kept falling, Nixon kept smiling.

He talked about marriage, but Pat didn't want to settle down. After a two-year courtship, however, she agreed to marry him. Pat had more money saved than he did, so she chipped in to buy her own ring and a new Oldsmobile. The wedding took place on June 21, 1940, at Mission Inn in Riverside, California. He wore a new suit, and she wore a light blue dress. For their honeymoon, they headed to Mexico. They had no hotel reservations and took along much of their own canned food to save money. As a joke, however, their friends had taken all the labels off the cans. Every meal became a game of chance, whether it was beans for breakfast or grapefruit slices for dinner.

Not long after they were married, the United States entered World War II. Richard wanted to help in the war effort, but the Quakers did not believe in fighting wars. He found another way to participate by taking a job with the Office of Price Administration, or OPA, in Washington, D.C. He and Pat moved to the nation's capital. His job was in the tire rationing section. It was boring, with lots of paperwork.

A year later, Nixon decided to join the Navy. He did not really agree with the Quakers' views on fighting, and he was already beginning to think of running for political office. He felt that being able to say he had served in World War II would help his chances. His choice greatly upset his mother and grandmother.

Nixon had led a relatively sheltered life before the Navy. In Whittier, no one smoked, drank, gambled, or cursed. It was quite a different story in the Navy. Away from their families, the lonely men passed their spare time drinking and playing cards. Nixon became very adept at poker. He was particularly good at bluffing, or making the other players think he had better cards than he had. But he missed Pat very badly. He wrote to her every day during the fourteen months he was away; Pat kept those letters for many years afterward.

Although he spent time in the Pacific Islands in areas close to battles, Nixon was not called upon to participate in combat. He mainly supervised the loading and unloading of planes. Sometimes the men worked sixteen hours straight, carrying thousands of pounds of cargo. Nixon worked along side them, even though as an officer he did not have to. His team spirit made him popular among his men.

Although his experience in World War II was disappointing, Richard Nixon had done what the Navy asked of him, and he had gained experience as a leader. He also befriended and grew to respect men from all walks of life, whether they were farm boys from Nebraska or sons of railroad engineers from New York. He felt a real kinship to hard-working, middle-class Americans, something he would never forget during his political career.

# Chapter Three

## Tricky Dick

In 1946, after his discharge from the Navy, Richard and Pat Nixon were expecting their first child. Richard was also ready to make his first run for political office.

A group of prominent Republicans in the 12th District of California, who called themselves the Committee of 100, asked him to run for the U.S. House of Representatives for the 12th District. Nixon jumped at the opportunity. His opponent, Democrat Jerry Voorhis, was not going to be easy to beat, however. Voorhis was very popular and had been elected to the House five times. He was voted the most honest congressman by the Washington, D.C. press, as well as the most hardworking congressman.

Richard had not been home long enough to begin earning money. The Nixons were living on the money they had saved during Nixon's time with the OPA and the Navy. There was little money to run a campaign. Pat was the only full-time campaign worker in the small office they rented for his headquarters. She spent hours typing up literature, stuffing envelopes, and carrying the mail to the post office. The campaign took its toll on her. As her pregnancy progressed, it became harder to smile and shake hands for hours on end at campaign rallies. One day she worked frantically to get some campaign literature ready to be mailed, only to discover there was no money to buy stamps. Another time she was suckered by an old political trick. Some people pretending to be Nixon supporters came into the office and said they wanted literature to hand out. Pat enthusiastically gave it to them, only to discover later that they were Voorhis supporters who threw all of it away.

Pat worked until just four days before she gave birth to a daughter, Patricia. She went back to work three days later. Although she would say later that this was not the life she had envisioned for herself, she believed very strongly that a woman should support her husband.

Nixon was still shy and awkward and had an annoying habit of not looking people in the eye when he was talking to them. But he did have a talent for persuasion. Even if a voter had different opinions, Nixon could somehow bring him or her around to his side.

Richard ran on a platform of less government regulation. He was also against labor unions and communism. This particularly appealed to voters in 1946, who were watching fearfully as the Soviet Union occupied the Eastern European nations, recently freed from Germany during World War II. The communists controlled the economy, owned all the factories, and restricted the media from reporting anything negative about the government. Communist troops sometimes used violence against people who did not want to go along with their policies.

These were frightening issues, and Nixon was quick to use voters' fears in his campaign. In his first run for political office, Nixon began to show what many viewed as a disturbing side of his personality. He did not simply want to win. He seemed to *need* to win, and was apparently willing to do or say what it took to assure victory. Soon, he resorted to negative campaigning. Although that is common today, it was not in the 1940s. Nixon was one of the first to use such tactics. Nixon the politician turned out to be a quite different person than the devout Quaker and quiet, hard-working student.

Voorhis was caught totally off-guard when, during a debate in a high school gym, Nixon suddenly accused him of being a communist sympathizer. Nixon said that of a list of forty issues, on which Voorhis had voted in the House, he had usually voted the way the communists would have preferred. When Voorhis stammered that he wanted to see the list, Nixon strode confidently across the stage and flashed a piece of paper.

To Voorhis' dismay, it was a list that greatly distorted his voting

This photograph of Pat Nixon was taken while Richard was serving in the U.S. Navy during World War II.

record. The issues Nixon cited were Voorhis' yes votes on such things as school-lunch programs and a loan to Great Britain to rebuild the massive damage it had suffered in World War II. These issues had nothing to do with communism—in fact, the U.S. Communist Party had opposed the loan to Britain. Nixon had even counted some of Voorhis' votes twice to arrive at the total of forty.

Toward the end of the campaign, Democrats in the 12th District began getting strange phone calls. A voice would say, "Did you know that Jerry Voorhis is a communist?" and hang up. Nixon and his supporters denied having anything to do with the calls and said perhaps the Democrats themselves made them, hoping Nixon would be blamed. But one woman claimed that she had been hired by the Nixon campaign to make the calls. Some who knew Nixon blamed his campaign advisor, Murray Chotiner, a large, outspoken man, for the negative campaign. Others, however, said that Nixon himself was very much in charge of his own campaign.

Voorhis never recovered from the political attacks. A politician from a different era, he was uncomfortable in such a battle. His aides begged him to retaliate in kind, but his efforts seemed weak and petty in the face of Nixon's volatile incriminations.

1946 was a good year to be a Republican. The Democratic Party had led the country through the Great Depression of the 1930s and World War II. Many thought it was time for a change. In the end, voters in the 12th District liked Nixon's platform of less government regulation and the hard line on communism. They gave him his first political victory.

The Nixons, with their new daughter, moved to Washington, D.C. They had little money and rented a small apartment. Then, Richard did what he had always done before. He got down to work.

Nixon quickly gained influence in the House. He helped to pass the Taft-Hartley Bill, which said that if a company's workers went on strike, it could hire new people to fill their positions. The bill also required union leaders to swear that they were not communists.

Nixon was one of nineteen congressmen chosen to visit Greece, Turkey and other countries in Europe to study the damage World War II had caused. He and the other travelers were to prepare a report on

Newly elected Congressman Richard Nixon with Pat and one-year-old
Tricia bicycling around the tidal basin in Washington, D.C.

a recommendation made by Secretary of State George Marshall to help rebuild the war-ravaged continent. The Marshall Plan called for millions of dollars of aid to help these countries get back on their feet. Before Nixon even left on the trip, however, he received a letter from six of the men who had been members of the Committee of 100 in California. They made it clear that they were in favor of lower taxes, less government and a balanced budget. This did not include sending millions of dollars to Europe. Their message was clear. The freshman representative should return home and vote against the Marshall Plan. The plan was also unpopular among average voters. Most people simply wanted to forget Europe and take care of problems closer to home.

The European trip, however, was a sobering one for Nixon. He saw millions of poor people on the verge of starvation and London's crumbled, bombed-out buildings. Nixon knew that if nothing were done to help Europe recover, the suffering people would turn to dictators offering simple answers. He became convinced that not supporting the Marshall Plan would play into the plans of the Soviets.

Nevertheless, the plan was still highly unpopular among the voters back in California. Nixon wrote columns for California newspapers and made speeches on why the Marshall Plan was necessary. Without help from the United States, he said, the governments of Europe would fall to chaos and communist revolution. He also convinced other Republicans to support Democratic President Harry Truman and vote yes on the plan. In the end, the Marshall Plan won approval from Congress.

The fight over the Marshall Plan opened a new chapter in Nixon's life. It was his first introduction to international relations. It also marked him as a different type of Republican. Previously, most members of his party had been isolationists. This meant they did not want the U.S. to become involved in international relations. Nixon made it clear during this controversy that it was possible to be a Republican and advocate that America take a more active role in foreign affairs.

In 1948, Nixon was easily reelected to a second term in Congress. The same year, Pat gave birth to their second daughter, whom they named Julie. Nixon kept up an exhausting schedule, though, and he took little time to spend at home with his growing family.

Nixon resented Alger Hiss's Ivy League education and his friendships with powerful people. He was determined to prove that Hiss was a communist.

For most Americans, 1948 was another frightening year. It became clear that the Soviets were developing their own atomic bomb, and they sent troops to take over the country of Czechoslovakia. Americans grew more afraid of communists here at home, too. Nixon, seeing an opportunity to enhance his stature, became a member of the House Committee on Un-American Activities that held hearings to question people accused of being communist sympathizers. Democrats, however, said the committee was accusing people falsely and drumming up hysteria. President Truman wanted to abolish the committee altogether.

One of the people the committee investigated was Alger Hiss, the president of the prestigious Carnegie Foundation for International Peace. During the Roosevelt administration, Hiss had worked for the State Department. He had accompanied Roosevelt to the Yalta Conference in 1945, where the president, British Prime Minister Winston Churchill, and Soviet leader Josef Stalin had discussed their post-war relationship. After the war, he had been in charge of setting up the new United Nations. In many ways, Hiss reminded Nixon of the Franklins, the well-established students he had despised back at Whittier College. Now Hiss was accused of being a communist.

A tall, elegant, well-educated man, Hiss had powerful friends in both the Democratic and Republican parties. His accuser was Whittaker Chambers, an overweight, rumpled editor at *Time* magazine. Chambers said that in the 1930s he and Hiss had been members of a secret group of the Communist Party.

Hiss denied everything. He told the committee that he did not even remember a man named Whittaker Chambers, and had never been a member of the Communist Party. His testimony was so eloquent that the room broke into applause when he finished.

Everyone seemed to believe Hiss—except Richard Nixon. After the hearing, he pointed out that Hiss never really denied knowing Chambers—he said only that he did not *remember* meeting him. Meanwhile, the House Committee on Un-American Activities was getting a lot of bad publicity, and the other congressmen pressured Nixon to drop the case. Nixon refused; he was determined to expose Hiss. But the public seemed to be against him, and the criticism began taking its toll on him.

At the beginning of the Hiss case, Nixon was the only congressman to believe the accusations made by Whittaker Chambers (left).

At his mother's house for dinner one night (his parents had moved east to be near him), he picked over his food, then paced the floor, deep in thought. Exasperated, Hannah Nixon finally said, "Richard, why don't you drop the case? No one else thinks Hiss is guilty. You are a young congressman. Older congressmen and senators have warned you to stop. Why don't you?"

"Mother, I think Hiss is lying," Nixon replied. "Until I know the truth, I've got to stick it out."

Then came the break Nixon had been waiting for. During a second round of questioning, Hiss seemed uncomfortable. Finally, he admitted that perhaps he had known Chambers after all—but under a different name, George Crosley.

Nixon then brought Chambers into the room and asked Hiss if he looked familiar. At first, Hiss didn't seem sure. He asked to examine Chambers' teeth, and he was allowed to do so, in front of the committee. Nixon was disgusted. He felt Hiss was putting on an act. Then, suddenly, Hiss proclaimed: "The ass under the lion's skin is Crosley. I have no further question at all. If he had lost both eyes and taken his nose off, I would be sure."

Nixon was now more convinced than ever that Hiss was lying. He also felt that he was close to proving it. In the next few weeks, Chambers testified that during the 1930s Hiss had stolen dozens of top-secret State Department documents. Sometimes he gave the documents to a photographer who took pictures of them. Other times Hiss gave papers to his wife, who would type copies. Then Hiss would put the originals back in their files and give the copies to Chambers, who passed them on to a Russian spy. Then, in another bizarre twist, Chambers led investigators out to a pumpkin patch behind his house. He reached inside a hollowed-out pumpkin and pulled out undeveloped rolls of microfilmed pictures of the documents that he said Hiss had stolen. This evidence came to be known as the "pumpkin papers."

At this point, most people became convinced Hiss had been a Soviet spy. Because more than ten years had passed since he allegedly stole the documents, Hiss was not tried for spying. But he was tried for perjury, or lying under oath. His first trial ended in a hung jury; at the second,

Although Nixon defeated Helen Gahagan Douglas in the 1950 race for senate from California, she pinned him with the life-long nickname of "Tricky Dick."

he was found guilty and sentenced to a prison term.

Millions of Americans followed the story of Nixon, Hiss, and Chambers in the newspapers and argued over Hiss' guilt or innocence. The case captured the imagination of the American people. The name "Richard Nixon" became a household word.

Despite his high popularity, Nixon still felt that he needed to run a negative campaign to win his next race. In 1950, he decided to run for the U.S. Senate. His opponent was Democrat Helen Douglas, a former actress who had also served in the House.

Nixon labeled Douglas the "Pink Lady." That was his way of linking her to the communists, who were often referred to as "Reds." Nixon said Douglas was "pink right down to her underwear." He and his supporters printed thousands of "pink sheets"—handouts that distorted Douglas' voting record.

Douglas had never been a popular representative. Nixon would have probably won without resorting to ugly tactics. In the end, he won the election by a large margin. But Douglas gained a certain measure of revenge. During the campaign she stuck Nixon with a nickname that would haunt him the rest of his life: "Tricky Dick."

Years later, Nixon said about his race with Douglas: "I'm sorry about that episode. I was a very young man."

Nixon's political career had been wildly successful, so far. Whether people liked him or not, Richard Nixon was building a solid reputation as an effective politician. In the Hiss case, he had stood up for what he believed. He had gained instant fame and respect among many Americans. It seemed that his path was unstoppable.

# Chapter Four

## A Dog Named Checkers

By 1952, Nixon was being talked about as a possible candidate for vice president of the United States. Just thirty-nine years old, his quick rise to power was an amazing accomplishment that few politicians have ever matched.

Earl Warren, the governor of California, was a possible candidate for the Republican nomination for president in 1952. He was counting on California Republicans, including Nixon, to support him. But Nixon told people privately that he didn't think Warren could win. The man he really wanted was General Dwight David "Ike" Eisenhower, the enormously popular commander of the allied forces in Europe during World War II. Nixon quietly helped change a policy at the Republican convention that summer that made it easier for Eisenhower to be nominated. For the rest of his life, Earl Warren, who later became Chief Justice of the U.S. Supreme Court, felt bitter toward what he viewed as Nixon's treachery.

When it came time for Eisenhower to choose a running mate, he remembered what Nixon had done for him. Nixon had many other things going for him, too. He had youth, experience, and contacts in both the House and the Senate. He was an excellent speaker with strong connections to both the conservative and liberal factions of the Republican Party. Nixon seemed like a perfect choice, although Eisenhower admitted that he did not much like Nixon personally.

Pat, however, was against the idea of Richard running a national campaign. She was tired of politics, and she knew that a run for vice president would be the toughest their family had faced yet. The two sat up late into the night, arguing about whether he should run.

Then the phone rang in the Nixons' room and Pat's arguments were quickly forgotten. One of Eisenhower's top advisors told Nixon, "We picked you." Nixon, overjoyed, threw on some clothes and rode in a limousine to Eisenhower's hotel for a middle-of-the-night meeting. "I'm glad you are going to be on the team, Dick. I think that we can win, and I know that we can do the right things for this country," Ike said.

Eisenhower told Nixon his expectations. The office of vice president was considered to be a mainly figurehead job with no real power or influence. Eisenhower said he wanted to change that. He would expect Nixon to be an active vice president. Nothing could have pleased Nixon more.

Eisenhower also made it clear that he wanted to stay above the negative attacks on the Democrats, but he very much wanted Nixon to continue them. This suited Nixon also.

Nixon enthusiastically took to the campaign trail. One of his main criticisms of the Democrats was corruption. President Harry Truman and his top aides, he charged, rewarded government officials for favors by giving them gifts like mink coats for their wives. These comments made the Democrats determined to find some dirt on Nixon, and they didn't have to look very far. Some of Nixon's fellow Republicans, angry with him for betraying Earl Warren, started a rumor that Nixon had an extra salary of about $18,000 paid by California millionaires.

When reporters questioned him about the fund, Nixon admitted that it existed. He explained that the money was not for him personally but was used to pay his campaign expenses, such as the cost of mailing campaign literature. In reality, $18,000 was not a large sum of money, even in 1952. The Nixons had a very modest lifestyle. Nixon's salary as a senator was $10,000 a year. Their home in Washington was an average one. Pat made her own curtains and slipcovers for the furniture.

Still, the rumors persisted. Even Republicans who Nixon had thought were his friends urged Eisenhower to drop him from the ticket. As Nixon rode around the country on a "whistle-stop" train tour, reporters hurled questions at him about the fund. Nixon answered that he was being persecuted by people who didn't like his anti-communist efforts.

Future Supreme Court Chief Justice Earl Warren (right) felt betrayed by Nixon after the 1952 Republican Convention.

Another explanation is probably closer to the truth: people, tired of his nasty campaigns, were getting back at him.

Eisenhower seemed to be effected by the criticism. He refused to take Nixon's phone calls and told reporters that he was taking his time deciding what to do about Nixon. One night at 2 a.m., a discouraged Nixon turned to Pat and said perhaps it was time for him to leave the ticket.

Although Pat had never wanted her husband to run for vice president, she had made up her mind to support him, and she was determined that Nixon should stay in the race. Eisenhower could not really afford to boot Nixon off the ticket, she said, because it would look as though he had made a bad choice. And Nixon owed it to their two daughters to defend himself. To do otherwise would tarnish the family's reputation forever. Her advice gave Nixon courage to keep going. He needed it badly. In Oregon, the crowds were hostile, even to the point of pushing and jostling Pat.

Finally, Eisenhower called, but he said little to reassure Richard. He told Nixon to take his case directly to the American people on national television. Eisenhower said he would make his decision based on how the public responded. Nixon thought that was cowardly, but he had little choice but to go along with what the general wanted.

Murray Chotiner, who was once again helping Nixon with the campaign, persuaded the Republican National Committee to put up the $75,000 to buy a half-hour of time on national television. As Nixon prepared for his speech, the media reported that Adlai Stevenson, the Democratic nominee for president, apparently had a fund of his own. The reporters, however, did not seem nearly as aggressive in questioning Stevenson about where the money had come from and what it was used for. Nixon was angry. He felt that the media was biased against him. He had a few reasons to feel hopeful, though. Two accounting firms had analyzed his funds and concluded that everything was legal.

Just hours before Nixon was to go on television, he received a phone call from Thomas Dewey, who had run against Truman in 1948 and was now a close associate of Eisenhower's. "There has just been a meeting of all of Eisenhower's top advisors," Dewey said, "and they have asked

Future Vice-President Nixon with future President Dwight Eisenhower at the 1952 Republican Convention.

me to tell you that it is their opinion that at the conclusion of the broadcast tonight you should submit your resignation to Eisenhower."

A furious Nixon shouted, "Just tell them that I haven't the slightest idea what I am going to do, and if they want to find out they'd better listen to the broadcast!" Then he slammed down the telephone.

The limousine ride to the television studio was deathly quiet. Nixon, Pat, and Chotiner arrived fifteen minutes before airtime, but even that short wait was excruciating. "I don't think I can go through with this one," he told Pat. "Of course you can," she replied, taking his hand and leading him onto the stage.

A few minutes later, Nixon and Pat, seated behind a desk, were on live television. "My fellow Americans," Nixon began, "I come before you tonight as a candidate for the vice presidency . . . and as a man whose honesty and integrity has been questioned." He repeated that not one penny of the $18,000 fund had ever gone to him, but only to pay political expenses "that I did not think should be charged to the taxpayers of the United States."

Then the camera showed handwritten lists of all of his finances. "It isn't very much, but Pat and I have the satisfaction that every dime that we've got is honestly ours. I should say this—that Pat doesn't have a mink coat. But she does have a respectable Republican cloth coat. And I always tell her that she'd look good in anything."

Finally, Nixon admitted he had accepted one gift from a supporter in Texas. "You know what it was? It was a little cocker spaniel in a crate that he had sent all the way from Texas. Black and white spotted. And our little girl—Tricia, the six-year-old—named it Checkers. And you know the kids love that dog and I just want to say this right now, that regardless of what they say about it, we're going to keep it."

Nixon walked around in front of the desk and continued talking. "And now, finally, I know that you wonder whether or not I am going to stay on the Republican ticket or resign. Let me say this: I don't believe that I ought to quit, because I am not a quitter. . . . The decision, my friends, is not mine. I would do nothing that would harm the possibilities of Dwight Eisenhower to become president of the United States, and

Pat on the television set with Nixon as he prepares to make the "Checkers speech" that saved his political career.

The Nixon family walking on the beach with Checkers, the little dog that Nixon insisted he would never give back.

for that reason I am submitting to the Republican National Committee tonight, through this television broadcast, the decision which it is theirs to make.... Wire and write ... whether you think I should stay or whether I should get off; and whatever their decision is, I will abide by it."

Immediately, the telephone switchboard at the network lit up with callers, most supporting Nixon. About fifty-eight million people had watched the broadcast, the largest television audience ever at that point in history. Two million telegrams and three million letters went to the Republican National Committee, the overwhelming majority supporting Nixon.

Eisenhower, too, sent a telegram to Nixon. It praised him for his speech but stopped short of endorsing him. He asked Nixon to fly to Wheeling, West Virginia, for a meeting. Nixon was furious and disappointed. He dictated to his secretary, Rose Mary Woods, a letter of resignation. Woods showed it to Chotiner, who tore it up. Nixon at first refused to go to Wheeling, but a friend persuaded him to go. After all,

Eisenhower was the general who had led the Allies to victory in Europe, and he was the boss in this presidential race.

As Nixon flew to Wheeling, a wire service reported that 107 of the 138 men on the Republican National Committee had voted to keep Nixon on the ticket. Eisenhower had apparently heard this, too. When the plane landed, he rushed up the steps to greet Nixon, his hand extended. "General, you didn't need to come out to the airport," Nixon said. "Why not?" Eisenhower grinned. "You're my boy."

But Nixon's broadcast, which would come to be known as the "Checkers speech," did not please everyone. Many thought it was shameful that Nixon had presented such personal details about his finances on national television. They thought the remarks about Pat's "respectable Republican cloth coat" and the little dog nauseating.

In the end, Eisenhower won the election easily. Nixon was now the second most powerful man in America. In his memoirs, Nixon wrote that the "fund crisis" was one of the biggest challenges of his life. "In politics, most people are your friends only as long as you can do something for them or something to them," he wrote. He added, "Still, I shall never forget my surprise and disappointment about those who turned against me overnight when it looked as if I would have to leave the ticket."

# Chapter Five

## Second In Command

President Eisenhower kept his promise to make Nixon an active vice president. He was aware of Nixon's interest in foreign affairs and wanted him to know the world's leaders, particularly those in Asia. During a seventy-day trip to nineteen countries, Richard and Pat visited Vietnam, Cambodia, and Burma, where he had a shouting match with a communist demonstrator in the street. During the trip, Nixon received much favorable press coverage, and Pat was popular with foreign leaders as well as the common people. When he returned home, however, Eisenhower did not seem interested in hearing much about the trip.

Nixon knew that if he wanted to be elected president he would need support in his own party. He became well-known for his tireless work on behalf of the Republican Party. He flew thousands of miles, even to desolate spots of Montana in the dead of winter, to campaign for Republicans running for the U.S. House of Representatives and the U.S. Senate. Sometimes he was the only well-known Republican that a candidate could count on to come speak on his behalf. Nixon's speeches usually had the same theme: that the Democrats were soft on communism. This message didn't win Nixon any friends among the Democrats, but many Republicans now owed him favors.

Despite Nixon's long, exhausting campaign trips, the election of 1954 proved disastrous for the Republican Party, which lost its majority in both the Senate and the House. That same year, the faculty of Duke University, where Nixon had received his law degree, voted sixty-one to forty-two against giving him an honorary doctorate, which indicated just how many people in the country did not like or trust him. Nixon had been scheduled to speak at Duke's graduation, but, humiliated, he canceled the speech. He was beginning to pay the price for his "take no prisoners" style of political campaigning.

One day, when he was discouraged that Eisenhower did not seem to want his advice and felt that the attacks on him were unfair, Nixon handed Murray Chotiner a folder of papers. "Here's my last campaign speech," he said. "It's the last one, because after this I am through with politics."

Then, in September 1955, Eisenhower suffered a heart attack. Nixon held temporary control of the country. Those who were looking for Nixon to come on too strong, to give the appearance of seizing power prematurely, were disappointed. Most of those who worked with him agreed that he conducted himself in a restrained and wise manner during Ike's illness.

As the 1956 election approached, some speculated that Eisenhower would not seek re-election because of his health. When he declared that he would run again, a rumble went through the nation. If Eisenhower were to die during his second term in office, Nixon would become president. There were many Democrats, and even some Republicans, who found that idea frightening.

Then, Eisenhower had another serious illness and was again hospitalized. The calls for the president to "dump Nixon" grew louder. The controversy continued right through the Republican convention that summer.

During the convention, Nixon's father, Frank, fell terribly ill. Richard and Pat flew to California to see him. From inside his oxygen tent, in terrible pain, Frank Nixon insisted that Richard go back to the convention in San Francisco. "You get back there, Dick, and don't let (them) pull any more last-minute funny business on you." He seemed to rally as he watched on television as the convention delegates chose Eisenhower and Nixon to run again. A relieved Nixon flew back to the convention to give his acceptance speech. Frank Nixon died a few days later.

Once again, Adlai Stevenson was Eisenhower's opponent, and, once again, Eisenhower defeated him handily with fifty-seven percent of the vote.

Less than a year after his reelection, Eisenhower suffered a stroke. Many people were sure this time that this was the end of Ike. Some even called for him to resign. To everyone's amazement, Eisenhower recovered very quickly. Just four days after his stroke, he took his wife, Mamie, to a church service.

In 1958, during his second term as vice president, Nixon took another trip abroad, this time to Latin America. During these years, the United States was unpopular there because Eisenhower had a reputation for supporting anti-communist dictators. Eisenhower and Nixon supported the overthrow of Jacabo Guzman in Guatemala in 1954.

On their Latin America trip, Nixon and Pat faced angry mobs. In Peru, the crowds hurled oranges, bottles, and rocks. Nixon lost his composure, jumped on top of a car, and shouted at the crowd that they were cowards. As a translator told the crowd in Spanish what Nixon had said, the mob grew uncontrollable. This was an unforgivable insult to the Peruvian people. The motorcade drivers turned the limousine around and rushed the Nixons to their hotel. As Nixon got out of the car, a man spat in his face. Nixon kicked him in the shin.

In Venezuela, Nixon and Pat were covered by a shower of spit as they made their way from the plane to the limousines. As Pat rode in a limousine behind Nixon's, she watched, fearfully, as men ripped the flags off of her husband's car, kicked its fenders and doors, and beat it with sticks and pipes, smashing the windows. One of his aides reached for his pistol, but Nixon stopped him. Firing a gun, he said, would give the mob an excuse to kill all of them. After twelve excruciating minutes, the Venezuelan police fired tear gas that dispersed the crowd.

Back home in the United States, some newspapers criticized Nixon for foolishly provoking the crowds. But the Republicans emphasized Nixon's bravery in standing up to communist demonstrators. 100,000 cheering people lined the streets to see him and Eisenhower ride from the airport to the White House.

American fear and distrust of the Soviet Union continued, but by

1959, Eisenhower and Nixon were making attempts to come to a better understanding with the new Soviet premier, Nikita Kruschev. Americans hoped that by warming up relations with Kruschev, the Soviets might even be convinced that democracy was a better way of life. As a first step, Nixon and Pat were to travel to the Soviet Union.

In Moscow, Nixon soon discovered that any effort to talk Kruschev out of being a communist was useless. After all the normal pleasantries had been exchanged and the two men sat down to talk privately, Kruschev wasted no time lashing out in anger at Nixon. He was particularly upset that the U.S. Congress had passed the Captive Nations Resolution, which called for a Captive Nations Week during which all Americans were asked to pray for people living under communist tyranny. Kruschev, red-faced, shouted to Nixon that it was stupid and insulting for Americans to think that Russian people were "captives."

The Nixon-Kruschev meetings were the top news story for the American and Russian press for days. A crowd of reporters followed them everywhere. Their most famous argument occurred as the two men toured an American exhibition designed to show the Russian people a typical American house with its modern appliances. In the kitchen area, they argued with each other about which way of life was best. Kruschev said the American exhibits did not impress the Russians. He argued that in Russia the communist system provided everyone with a house, while in America, only people who had enough money for a house could own one. "And you say *we* are slaves!" he said. In Russia, the government oversaw the building of all houses and the production of such items as washing machines, and there was not much variety of products from which to choose. Kruschev said the American system of producing many different types of houses and washing machines was inefficient.

Nixon replied: "To us, diversity, the right to choose, the fact that we have a thousand different builders, that's the spice of life. We don't want to have a decision made at the top by one government official saying that we will have one type of house. That's the difference."

As the men continued around the exhibition, their debate continued, even to the point where photographers captured them jabbing their fingers at each other. Although their exchange in the "Kitchen Debate" appeared tense, Kruschev was smiling at the end, for the premier, like Nixon, enjoyed a good, spirited argument, especially in front of an audience of millions.

While in Russia, Nixon was allowed to address a gathering of Russians who had come to see the exhibit, a speech that was printed in full in two Russian newspapers. He also became the first American leader to talk directly to the Soviet people on television. The government controlled the media. Much of the news it reported about America was censored or distorted. Nixon's speeches were a rare opportunity for an American to break through that censorship.

Nixon used these opportunities to tell not only about the millions of Americans who owned television sets, cars and houses, but to talk about the American philosophies of freedom of religion and freedom of the press. He explained that Americans, unlike Russians, did not need permits or passports to travel within their own country. He told the Russians that much of what Premier Kruschev said was reported in the American press, while almost none of President Eisenhower's words ever reached the Russian people.

On their way home, Nixon and Pat passed through Warsaw, Poland, which had been divided between Germany and the Soviet Union at the end of World War II. An uprising of the Polish people against the communist government had been quashed by the Soviets. In stark contrast to the rocks and spit that had greeted them in Latin America, the Nixons were deeply moved by the reception they received from the Poles. Although the government had tried to keep their visit quiet, millions lined the streets to cheer wildly. Bouquets of flowers rained down on the Nixons' open cars. When Kruschev had toured Poland just weeks before, the government handed out flowers to be thrown. As the Nixons rode through the city, however, the Polish people yelled, "This time we bought our own flowers!"

One result of the trip was that Nixon realized that Kruschev was firmly set in his convictions that communism was a superior system. The experience had a profound effect on Nixon. In the coming years, he would have many opportunities to meet with communist leaders, but he had learned that arguing with them about their system of government

Nixon gained acclaim for his tough exchanges with Soviet Premier
Nikita Khrushev during a visit to Moscow in 1959.

was a waste of his breath.

His travels abroad were setting the stage for his next step in political life. Nixon had put in his time as vice president, and now he was ready to try for the highest office in the land—the presidency of the United States.

# Chapter Six

## Two Heartbreaking Races

President Eisenhower could not run for reelection in 1960. It was Nixon's turn to try to win the office for himself. He easily won the Republican nomination. After much struggle among several Democrats, the party nominated Senator John F. Kennedy of Massachusetts to be their candidate for President.

Kennedy's background was much different from Nixon's. He came from a family of tremendous wealth and influence and had been educated in the finest prep schools and Ivy League universities. He had never had to do hard, manual labor and was a handsome, photogenic man with a lovely, pregnant young wife. He laughed at himself easily and had a good sense of humor, while Nixon seemed self-conscious and awkward. Although Kennedy was only four years younger than Nixon, he looked much younger.

Nixon had one great advantage. His years as vice president meant he was much better known to the American people than Kennedy. For that reason, Nixon's campaign advisers told him not to accept Kennedy's challenge to a series of television debates. Nixon did not need the exposure, so the debates would help Kennedy more. Nixon, however, could not resist the idea of debating on television. After all, his televised Checkers speech had saved his career, and he had been a champion debater. He was certain he could best Kennedy in a face-off.

Nixon threw himself into the campaign. He promised to visit all fifty states before the election. One thing he did not plan on was getting hurt or sick. That summer of 1960, while campaigning in Greensboro, North

Carolina, Nixon bumped his knee on a car door. It seemed like a minor injury, but the knee grew swollen and painful and he could no longer place any weight on it. Finally, Nixon's doctor put him in the hospital. Nixon had a life-threatening infection, and there was a chance his leg might have to be amputated. He had no choice but to spend two agonizing weeks on his back pumped full of antibiotics. Meanwhile, Kennedy was drawing big crowds everywhere he went.

Nixon's bad luck continued. Eisenhower hesitated to openly support his vice president. Having the endorsement of the president for whom he had worked eight years was crucial, and Nixon's experience as a vice president was his key selling point in the campaign. However, when reporters questioned Eisenhower about what decisions he might have made based on Nixon's advice, he stumbled and could not name one. As the reporters kept pressing, he finally blurted out, "If you give me a week, I might think of one. I don't remember." He realized at once that what he had said would hurt Nixon, and he called him right away to apologize. The damage had already been done, however.

Nixon resumed his whirlwind tour of the country as soon as he was out of the hospital. Then he came down with the flu, but refused to cancel any speeches or to back away from his pledge to visit all fifty states.

By the first debate on September 26 Nixon had lost so much weight his shirt collar hung loose around his neck, but he refused to buy a better-fitting shirt for the television debate. He looked pale and sickly, and his dark beard always made him look unshaven even a few hours after he had shaved, but he refused makeup. On his way to the studio, he banged his knee again. He didn't complain, but it was obvious he was in pain. Unfortunately, both candidates had to stand throughout the telecast.

In contrast, Kennedy looked healthy, tanned, and fit. The appearances were deceiving, however. Nixon was actually much healthier than Kennedy, who had several chronic health problems, including a bad back and a long-time battle with a glandular disease.

There was nothing fateful or very memorable said during the debate that night. Both candidates came across well. But history was made. Many now point to to this debate as the moment when television began controlling the American political system.

The audience that heard the debate on the radio said they thought Nixon won. His answers were deemed clearer and more insightful. Those that saw the event on television, however, had quite a different perspective. Immediately after the broadcast, Nixon's secretary, Rose Mary Woods, got a call from her parents. They wanted to know if Nixon was feeling well. That became the general consensus, especially among the writers and television reporters who helped determine the winner. Kennedy had won because he came across on television as the most relaxed with the medium.

It became clear that television was a whole new ball game in political campaigns. The Kennedy-Nixon debate became a landmark case in showing how appearances mattered at least as much—if not more—than substance.

Nixon learned his lesson, and in the subsequent television debates with Kennedy he wore make-up and looked well-groomed and re-freshed. Unfortunately, not as many people watched. While eighty million viewers saw the first face-off, only sixty million watched the second.

By October, the race was too close to call. This was gong to finish as one of the closest races ever. Eisenhower, who disliked Kennedy, finally hit the campaign trail for Nixon. As soon as the president entered the fray, it became clear that he was a tremendous asset. He drew huge, cheering crowds everywhere he went.

Then, eight days before the election, Nixon got a call from Eisenhower's wife, Mamie. She begged Nixon to stop Ike from cam-paigning. She was afraid that his health would not hold up. She begged Nixon not to tell Ike that she had called; she had already tried, unsuccessfully, to talk him out of the speeches.

Nixon met with Eisenhower. Ike began telling Nixon of all the places he planned to speak on his behalf. Nixon awkwardly made excuses for why Eisenhower shouldn't go. Eisenhower was hurt and angry. He thought Nixon was rejecting his help. But Nixon said nothing about Mamie's phone call.

Nixon missed an opportunity to make a positive impact on his campaign when, on October 19, 1960, the civil rights leader Martin

Luther King Jr. was arrested during a sit-in in a department store in Atlanta. The judge, after seeing that King was already on probation for driving without a valid license, sentenced him to four months in prison. Many blacks and whites feared he would be killed before he was ever released. Most everyone thought the sentence was racially motivated.

Nixon was a friend of King, and King had endorsed the Republicans in 1956. Nixon had a good record on civil rights. He had frequently said in speeches that America could not hold itself up as an example of freedom to communist countries if it was guilty of racism at home. When someone suggested that Nixon use his influence to get King out of prison, however, Nixon balked, saying that would be going too far.

This decision was a mistake. Kennedy's brother, Robert Kennedy, who managed the Kennedy campaign, called the Atlanta judge and talked him into releasing King on bond. King's father, Martin Luther King Sr., had endorsed Nixon, but now he felt that he should tell millions of blacks to vote for Kennedy. Two million pamphlets endorsing Kennedy were distributed in black churches.

The final blow to the Nixon campaign came in the days before the election when the press reported that Nixon's brother, Donald, had received a $205,000 loan from billionaire Howard Hughes. The loan was to save his failing grocery store and gas station, but the press reported that Hughes had received some favors, including a tax break, in exchange.

Despite these setbacks for Nixon, the race was still too close to call going into Election Day. Even at 11:30 p.m., Nixon, watching the returns on television, calculated that if he won Illinois and Minnesota, he might still have a chance. As midnight approached, however, he and Pat went downstairs in the hotel to tell a crowd that he might lose. Someone in the crowd shouted, "No, no, don't concede!" Pat began crying, and Nixon, in a rare public display of affection, put his arm around her.

After only a few hours' sleep, Nixon rose to find that he had lost by the narrowest margin in history. The American public was split almost fifty-fifty between him and Kennedy. But the election is truly decided in the Electoral College, where a group of people equal to the number of members each state has in the U.S. Congress cast their votes for the

This first debate between Nixon and John F. Kennedy was a watershed event in American politics. In the future, every candidate would pay close attention to how they appeared on television.

one candidate who won the popular vote in their state. Hence, Kennedy led the Electoral College vote 303-219. For Nixon, it was a heartbreaking loss.

For the rest of his life, Nixon and his supporters would ask, "What if?" What if Eisenhower had campaigned those last few days? What if Nixon had helped King get out of jail? Another big question concerned Texas and Illinois, where there was evidence of voter fraud. Kennedy's father, Joseph Kennedy, was known as a sharp businessman. Some speculated that he had used his vast resources to alter the vote counts in several large cities, especially Chicago, where the powerful Mayor Dailey was a Kennedy supporter.

Because of the close election results, Nixon could have demanded a recount of all the votes by hand, but he chose not to. In the days before computers, such a task could have taken a year and a half. Who would have served as president in the meantime? Nixon decided it would be too disruptive and traumatic for the country. In his view, America could not afford to have its own government in chaos.

After Kennedy's inauguration, Nixon, Pat, and the girls moved from Washington to California. He had been the most involved, visible and effective vice president of the twentieth century, but he was also a highly divisive figure. People either loved or hated Richard Nixon. To those who supported him, Nixon was an intelligent man of virtue, integrity, and common sense. He stood up to Kruschev and to communism. To those who hated him, he was "Tricky Dick," the mastermind of nasty campaigns. Their cartoons showed him as a dark, mean little man who climbed out of sewers.

Nixon picked up where he had left in 1946, practicing law in California. He could not get politics out of his blood, however. Nor would the Republicans let him. They saw an opportunity for Nixon in California—running against Governor Pat Brown in 1962.

Nixon knew this race would not be easy. Brown, a Democrat, was a popular governor who had made no real mistakes. He had made popular investments in education. The other problem for Nixon was that there were one million more Californians registered as Democrats than as Republicans. By 1962, Kennedy was an enormously popular president, and Democrats nationwide were faring well.

Some of the people Nixon trusted most advised him not to run. If he lost, they argued, he would truly appear washed up. His own family split on the issue. Pat, who had looked forward to a normal life, was against going through another race. Tricia sided with her mother. Julie encouraged her father to run.

In truth, Nixon did not feel very enthusiastic about being governor of California. He had loved the big stage of national and international politics. Serving as governor, even of a state as large as California, would be a let down.

Nixon wrestled with the decision. Then one night, as he wrote a statement saying that he had decided not to run, Pat came in. "I have thought about it some more," she said, "and I am more convinced than ever that if you run it will be a terrible mistake. But if you weigh everything and still decide to run, I will support your decision. I'll be there campaigning with you just as I always have." She kissed him and left the room.

Nixon tore up his speech and began writing the new one, saying he would run.

The campaign was, as usual in a campaign involving Nixon, a nasty one. The Howard Hughes loan to his brother, Donald, was an issue because Nixon was never able to satisfactorily explain it. But his biggest problem was Brown's charge that Nixon simply viewed being governor as a stepping-stone to another campaign for president, and that he would abandon his term halfway through to jump into the 1964 presidential race.

Nixon denied Brown's charge, but no one was convinced by his denial. The truth was that he did not relish the thought of another race against Kennedy, who appeared unbeatable. It didn't help support his argument when, while hosting a television show, Nixon mistakenly said, "When I become *president*..." then hastily corrected himself by saying, "When I become governor of the *United States*..." Brown immediately seized the opportunity to say he had been right about Nixon all along.

Nixon turned to his old campaign habit of saying that his Democratic opponent was "soft" on communism. This time, the voters did not believe it about Brown. Brown did not run a clean campaign, either. He said he was a "better American" than Nixon, and that he had "the most heart" of the two candidates.

The press reported all of the corny statements, and for the most part, both candidates got equally positive—and negative—coverage. Nixon was not used to this, however. In his past campaigns for the U.S. House and Senate, the *Los Angeles Times* and other large newspapers in the state had favored him over his Democratic opponents. What the reporters considered unbiased reporting Nixon considered unfair to him.

The election was a disaster for Nixon. He lost by 300,000 votes and, brimming over with anger and frustration, he took it out on the reporters at the "last press conference."

Although Nixon said during the tense news conference that he was quitting politics, those who knew him well never believed he would give up his dream of returning to the White House. But they all agreed it would take some time before he regained his respectability. No one could have guessed at the rapid change of circumstances that awaited the entire country—circumstances that would go a long way in giving Nixon an opportunity for a comeback. The immediate question for Nixon and his supporters was what would the former vice president do in the meantime.

# Chapter Seven

## Victory Out of Chaos

By 1963, President Kennedy was idolized by many Americans. Some complained, especially whites in the South, about Kennedy's support for civil rights. But he seemed to be assured of an easy win for reelection in 1964.

Then, on a sunny day in November 1963, Kennedy was shot in the head as he rode in an open-air car through downtown Dallas, Texas. A few days later, millions of mourners lined the streets of Washington to watch the horse-drawn carriage bearing his coffin roll slowly past. Millions more watched the funeral on television. The entire nation was stunned. The scene of Kennedy's toddler son, John F. Kennedy Jr., saluting his father's coffin as it passed by was forever stamped in the nation's memory. Vice President Lyndon B. Johnson, a former senator from Texas,was now the nation's new president.

With Kennedy gone, Nixon began hinting that he could be talked into running for president in 1964, but he did not actively pursue it. He knew that it would take time to refurbish his image. As he wrote later, "After 1960 and 1962, I had what every politician dreads most, a loser image. In fact, after the 'last press conference,' I had a *sore* loser image." In the end, the Republican nomination went to Barry Goldwater, who overwhelmingly lost to Johnson.

Although Americans had supported Eisenhower and Kennedy, most did not realize at the time the consequences of one aspect of their foreign policy. In the 1950s, Eisenhower had sent several hundred military advisors to South Vietnam to fight against the communist North

Vietnamese. Between 1961 and 1963, President Kennedy increased the number of Americans there from 900 to 16,000.

After the Kennedy assassination, during the years of increased military involvement in Vietnam, came a time of turmoil and change, much different than the 1950s, when Nixon had been vice president. Many of those who benefitted from the prosperity of the Eisenhower years were now angry and restless, especially the middle-class youth. Protests against the government and the war in Vietnam occurred on college campuses and in major cities.

Not all Americans had enjoyed the prosperity of the 1950s. Large numbers of African Americans continued to live in poverty. In the South and parts of the North, African Americans attended separate, inferior schools, and were forced to drink out of separate water fountains, sit in the back of city buses, and endure the humiliation of being treated like lesser humans than the white population. The eloquent Martin Luther King Jr. led a peaceful effort to combat these injustices. Malcolm X spoke for those who were impatient with the pace of King's non-violent tactics.

During the cultural revolution that accompanied anger against Vietnam, many youths rejected the traditional values their parents had held. They experimented with drugs. Women began to speak out for their right to work and to earn as much money as men did. While women of the 1950s had relished making a happy home for their husbands and children, younger women rejected that lifestyle and saw their mothers as victims.

In the midst of this turmoil, Richard and Pat moved their family to New York City. Nixon also had personal tragedies. His mother had a number of serious health problems. One day, when she was in terrible pain after surgery, Nixon had said, "Mother, don't give up."

Hannah pulled herself up in the bed and said, "Richard, don't *you* give up. Don't let anybody tell you that you are through."

Hannah had a stroke shortly after and spent the last two years of her life in a nursing home in Whittier, where she died in 1965. Among those who attended the funeral was the Rev. Billy Graham.

In New York, Nixon worked with the prestigious New York law firm of Mudge, Rose, Guthrie and Alexander—one of the firms that had turned down his job application when he was fresh out of law school. But he kept his fingers in politics. He wrote an autobiographical book, *Six Crises,* about the major struggles of his life. He continued traveling around the country, campaigning for Republicans.

By 1966, voters seemed to be losing their patience with the Johnson Administration. The turmoil in the streets and the slow, bloody pace of the Vietnam War frightened many people. They wanted to restore the country to the normalcy they remembered from the Eisenhower years. This made this election year a good one for Republicans. They won many additional seats in the U.S. House and Senate. Nixon made it a point to campaign for many of the party's candidates. Several of the victors felt that they owed their success to him.

In many of his 1966 speeches, Nixon criticized President Johnson's handling of the Vietnam struggle. Nixon said Johnson was not committing enough troops and ammunition to defeat the North Vietnamese. If Johnson would step up American efforts, he said, the war would be won.

This argument proved to be effective with voters. But, in reality, Johnson did send more and more troops to Vietnam. Eventually, the number reached 540,000. Americans had simply underestimated the iron will of the North Vietnamese, who rushed to train more men to replace the ones who had been killed in battle. No matter how many American men Johnson sent, the war continued. Back home in America, people became increasingly alarmed at the human toll of the fighting. It seemed that every night the network news reported that hundreds more young American men were dying. They began to question why America was in Vietnam in the first place. So what if the North Vietnamese took over the country and it became communist. Was it worth giving thousands of American lives to the cause? At college campuses nationwide, students staged sit-ins in classroom buildings and chanted criticisms of the American government. As the war continued, their protests grew more hostile.

The despair did not just touch young people. Their parents, many who remembered World War II, watched their sons and daughters on television every night burn the American flag and call police officers "pigs." It seemed that the country was coming apart at the seams.

In March of 1968, President Johnson announced that he would not run for reelection. Vice President Hubert H. Humphrey was now the most likely candidate for the Democrats. Nixon did not think Humphrey would be a strong candidate.

Nixon mulled over these realities as he looked at his chance to run for president in 1968. The country had certainly changed since 1960. It would be possible to present himself as a "New Nixon." He expressed sympathy for the older Americans who still believed America was a great country, a preserver of democracy, and a place of moral and religious values.

Pat did not want Richard to run. She liked her life in New York. They were a family; Nixon was earning a great deal of money. She did not understand Richard's ceaseless ambition. However, it soon became clear nothing was going to stop him from running. She had no choice but to give her blessing.

Nixon started the race by promising a return to law and order. "When the strongest nation in the world can be tied down for four years in the war in Vietnam with no end in sight," he said, "when the nation with the greatest tradition of respect for the rule of law is plagued by random lawlessness; when the nation that has been a symbol of human liberty is torn apart by racial strife; when the president of the United States cannot travel at home or abroad without fear of hostile demonstrations, then it is time America had new leadership!"

Nixon's campaign in 1968 was very different from his previous ones. Instead of an exhausting tour of all fifty states, Nixon's campaign adviser, Bob Haldeman, came up with a new strategy. Nixon taped "town meetings" to be shown on the air in which he answered questions from a mostly sympathetic audience. The advantage to this format was that it could be edited, which would cut down the risk of embarrassing blunders on Nixon's part. Reporters, most of whom Nixon still did not trust, had little access to him to ask the tough questions, such as exactly how he would end the Vietnam war. Tension between Nixon and the press continued to mount.

After Nixon entered the Republican primary, Senator Robert Kennedy,

President Lyndon Johnson saw his presidency undermined by the controversial Vietnam War.

brother of the dead president, announced he would run. Nixon feared reliving the agonizing loss to John Kennedy. Another opponent was Governor George Wallace of Alabama, who was running as an independent. Wallace appealed to Southern voters frightened by the move toward civil rights. His rallying cry was "Segregation now, segregation forever."

Then, on April 4, 1968, Martin Luther King Jr. was shot dead as he stood on a hotel balcony in Memphis. Rioting spread across the country. Nixon flew to Atlanta to pay his respects to Mrs. King and to talk with her about how much he had admired her husband. He was not going to make the same mistake he had made in 1960, when King was jailed in Atlanta.

Two months later, in June, Americans endured yet another unbelievable tragedy. As Robert Kennedy passed through a hotel kitchen in California, an assassin shot him. It seemed that American society was in a total upheaval. There was nothing left that Americans could believe in. These events tended to strengthen the law and order candidacy of Nixon.

During all this turmoil, a happy event was taking place in the lives of the Nixons. Daughter Julie, now nineteen, and David Eisenhower, Ike's grandson, began dating. Americans fell in love with the cute young couple. They were featured in many magazines, and they were a hit on the campaign trail for Nixon.

One nagging problem for the Nixon campaign was similar to 1960. Eisenhower, now very sick with heart trouble in Walter Reed Hospital in Maryland, had never publicly endorsed Nixon for the presidency. Nixon finally mustered his nerve to ask for his support. To his delight, Ike replied, "Dick, I don't want there to be any more question about this. You're my choice, period." A few days later, Eisenhower called a few reporters into his hospital room. In a weak voice, clothed in a bathrobe, he read a statement from his wheelchair that he would support Nixon for president because of his "intellect ... decisiveness, warmth, and above all, his integrity."

Nixon won the Republican nomination at the convention that summer. At 11 p.m. the night of his nomination, Nixon appeared on the

The streets of Chicago erupted into a full-scale riot after police and anti-war demonstrators clashed on during the 1968 Democratic Convention.

podium. The applause in the arena was deafening. Nixon raised his arms above his head and smiled. The crowd roared. At the end of his acceptance speech, he proclaimed, "And I say let's win this one for Ike." The audience went wild.

Nixon chose Spiro Agnew, the governor of Maryland, to be his vice presidential running mate. Agnew was not well known, but he had a reputation for upholding law and order. Nixon thought this position would appeal to voters, especially Southerners.

Nixon was helped by what happened the following month in Chicago, where the Democratic Convention erupted in riots. Thousands of angry young people surrounded the convention center, protesting the war. The Chicago police angrily tried to break up the crowds. The protesters yelled "Pigs!" and blew marijuana smoke in the faces of the police. The police began shoving and beating, then fired tear gas into the crowd. Television cameras captured the melee. "The whole world is watching! The whole world is watching!" the crowd yelled.

Nothing was peaceful inside the convention hall, either. Hubert Humphrey was nominated, though the Democrats were badly divided in their views on the war. The convention was such an embarrassing mess that even the Democrats felt they had just handed the election to Richard Nixon.

President Johnson now realized he must try to end the war as soon as possible. In his last months in office, he began trying to negotiate with North Vietnam. But the North Vietnamese balked; they knew that they were winning and had no incentive to negotiate. South Vietnam, dependent on American troops, did not want the United States to withdraw either. This left Johnson in a terrible position. If he simply pulled out the troops, he would be the first American president to lose a war. America had always been the world's great defender of democracy. How could this great nation admit that it could not defeat the communists in a small country like Vietnam?

Nixon worried that Johnson might end the war quickly to help Vice President Humphrey win the election. He asked a friend, John Mitchell, to call Mrs. Anna Chan Chennault, a Chinese woman who was the widow of a great wartime general. Mitchell asked Mrs. Chennault to call

President Nguyen Van Thieu of South Vietnam and tell him *not* to go to the peace talks Johnson was trying to arrange. He asked her to assure Thieu that he would get a better deal from Nixon once he was elected. Mitchell had to be careful what he said, however, because he knew that President Johnson had asked the FBI to tap Mrs. Chennault's telephone. In fact, Nixon discovered that his own campaign plane had been bugged, too.

Thieu did indeed refuse to go to the negotiations, although it is not clear that Nixon and Mrs. Chennault had anything to do with it. He had never wanted to negotiate with the North Vietnamese anyway. And even though Johnson knew Nixon was trying to sabotage his peace talks, he could not tell the public about it because he would have had to admit that he had tapped Mrs. Chennault's phone.

All three presidential candidates—Nixon, Humphrey, and Wallace—endured heckling from protestors. None had specific plans for ending the war. They simply told the voters what they knew they wanted to hear.

Election Day provided another close Nixon election. This time it was a reversal of the 1960 loss to Kennedy. Humphrey actually won the popular vote by a narrow margin, but Nixon won the Electoral College votes—and the presidency.

At noon the next day in New York, Nixon appeared before a hotel ballroom full of cheering supporters. "Having lost a close one eight years ago and having won a close one this year, I can say this—winning's a lot more fun."

He added, "I saw many signs in this campaign. Some of them were not friendly and some were very friendly. But the one that touched me the most was the one that I saw in Deshler, Ohio. A teenager held up a sign, 'Bring Us Together.' And that will be the great objective of this administration at the outset, to bring the American people together."

By Inauguration Day, Nixon knew bringing the country together was going to be a difficult task. As he rode down Pennsylvania Avenue to the White House on a gray, dreary January 20, 1969, sticks, stones and beer cans rained on his car. Those in the crowd who did not believe his promise to end the war chanted, "Four more years of death!" Only time would tell if they were right.

# Chapter Eight

## President Nixon

Christmas 1968 was an especially joyful one for the Nixons. They would be inaugurated the next month as the First Family and, on December 22, Julie Nixon and David Eisenhower were married. Although they had said they wanted an intimate, personal ceremony, this proved to be impossible for the daughter of America's new president-elect and the grandson of a former president. Every detail of the wedding plans, from the design of the bride's dress to what Pat would wear, was published in magazines nationwide.

There were sad moments, too. Two months after Nixon became president Dwight Eisenhower died. Standing before the coffin in the rotunda of the U.S. Capitol in Washington, his voice brimming with emotion, Nixon told those who had gathered for the funeral that Eisenhower "was one of the giants of our time." Eisenhower was "loved by more people in more parts of the world than any president America has ever had."

The most pressing problem Nixon faced was the Vietnam War. Nixon suspected that the young college students protesting were mostly angry because they were the ones being drafted. He announced that he would ask Congress to declare all young men, ages twenty and over, to be free from the draft. The protests declined.

Unfortunately, the peace on college campuses didn't last long into his presidency. Nixon soon learned that North Vietnam was sending supplies to its troops from positions in Cambodia. Nixon ordered bombings of those supply lines. To keep the bombings secret, he did not even notify Secretary of State William Rogers, the man who was supposed to be his top advisor on foreign policy. To most presidents, making such an important decision without notifying key people would have been out of the question. It was clear from the beginning that Nixon would be a very controlling and secretive president.

The bombings were secret for only a short time—until the *New York Times* published a story about them. College campuses again erupted in protest. Nixon was enraged. He believed someone on his staff must have leaked the story to the press. He told Henry Kissinger, his national security adviser, who was emerging as his top adviser on foreign policy, to give J. Edgar Hoover, the head of the FBI, the names of seventeen people on the White House and National Security staffs. Nixon thought these might be the people passing information to the press. Hoover was ordered to place taps on their telephones. Nixon even added his own brother, Donald. Nixon had learned that sometimes Donald would ask people for business loans and promise them that his powerful brother would do them a favor in return.

*The New York Times* published a series of stories about the top-secret "Pentagon Papers," an account of America's involvement in Vietnam through the Johnson administration. The articles caused a big stir because they showed that Kennedy and Johnson had deliberately deceived the public. At first, Nixon paid little attention. After all, the Pentagon Papers had nothing to do with him. But Kissinger threw a fit. "The fact that some idiot can publish all of the diplomatic secrets of this country on his own is damaging to your image, as far as the Soviets are concerned, and it could destroy our ability to conduct foreign policy," Kissinger said.

Kissinger knew just how to convince Nixon to react to the Pentagon Papers. He added, "It shows you're a weakling, Mr. President." It worked. Nixon called in John Ehrlichman, his chief domestic adviser, and told him to stop the "leaks" at any cost. "I want you to set up a little group right here in the White House," he said. "Have them get off their tails and find out what's going on and figure out how to stop it."

Ehrlichman formed a group of men and gave them an office. They hung a sign on the door that read "Plumbers," because they were there to stop leaks. One of the "Plumbers" was a man named E. Howard Hunt, a former operative for the Central Intelligence Agency who was an expert in break-ins and spying. Nixon had several ideas for what Hunt and his men could do. He told Bob Haldeman, his chief of staff, to ask Hunt to break in to the Brookings Institution, a Washington, D.C. think tank. Nixon believed that some classified documents about Vietnam were housed there. "You talk to Hunt," Nixon said. "I want the break-in. Hell, they (Hunt and his friends) can do that. You're to break into the place, rifle the files, and bring them in."

While this illegal act was never carried out, the "Plumbers" did try another break-in. Daniel Ellsberg, a former member of the State Department, had given the Pentagon Papers to the press. Ellsberg was now America's newest celebrity. He was appearing on television talk shows, defending his part in publishing the secret documents. This enraged Nixon, who was angry that someone would get such positive publicity for stealing classified papers.

The "Plumbers" learned that Ellsberg had seen a psychiatrist. They broke into the psychiatrist's office to steal his records, hoping they would find evidence that the Soviets had paid Ellsberg to steal the documents. They found nothing to support this theory. The "Plumbers" continued to look for leakers and others they considered enemies of the Nixon administration.

While it is not clear if Nixon knew about the "Plumbers" activities, he had instigated the creation of the group and, with his own deep mistrust, had fostered an environment in which his men thought it was acceptable to break the law to do what he wanted.

Nixon was very concerned about his public image. He had his aides prepare for him, every day, a news summary of what all the major newspapers and television networks had said about him. Sometimes one day's news summary was fifty pages long, but Nixon read every word. He did not take criticism well. Whenever he read about someone who had made a negative comment, he would scrawl orders to his staff in the margins of the page: "Get someone to hit him," "cut him," "freeze him," or "dump him."

His staff wisely ignored most of these suggestions, but sometimes

Early in his presidency, National Security Advisor Henry Kissinger (right) became Nixon's top foreign policy advisor. Kissinger encouraged Nixon to begin wiretapping people he thought were giving information to the press.

they followed Nixon's orders. Nixon was especially eager to have the Internal Revenue Service investigate his Democratic opponents to see if they had by chance cheated on their taxes or done anything else that could be exposed to embarrass them. He even had someone follow Senator Ted Kennedy, the brother of the dead president, who was rumored to be a potential presidential candidate. "Who knows about the Kennedys?" Nixon said. "Shouldn't they be investigated?" The staff kept a "Freeze List," an "Opponents List" and an "Enemies List" of all the reporters, politicians and entertainers who were not to be told anything or invited to attend any White House functions.

The public, however, did not yet know what was going on inside the White House. Vietnam was first on everyone's mind. In the spring of 1969, Nixon flew to Midway Island in the Pacific Ocean to meet President Nguyen Van Thieu of South Vietnam. The two men announced "Vietnamization," a plan in which the Americans would train the South Vietnamese to gradually take over all the fighting themselves. Meanwhile, the American troops would be withdrawn in stages. Nixon announced that the first group of 25,000 American men would leave Vietnam very soon.

Although this was encouraging news, Nixon knew the whole truth and did not share it with the American people. The United States and South Vietnam were losing the war. How could he tell the men still there that more of them would die before the United States finished pulling out all of the troops? To simply pull all of them out at once would be to admit defeat. It would be an admission that the entire war had been a mistake. Nixon did not want to be president when the U.S. admitted to a defeat in a military conflict.

Even as he pulled out the ground troops, Nixon hoped to save face and force the North Vietnamese to negotiate an end to the war, so he stepped up the bombing from the air. Meanwhile, he reassured the public that his goal was to have all U.S. troops out of Vietnam by the end of 1970.

He did not fulfill that promise. In February 1970, the North Vietnamese stepped up their fighting in the neighboring country of Laos. Nixon sent in ground troops again.

Morale was terrible among the American men in Vietnam. Eighteen- and nineteen-year-olds were still being sent to fight, sometimes without adequate training. Many turned to drugs as an escape from the horrors of a war where no one was sure who was the enemy. In fact, there were more American soldiers addicted to heroin than were killed in the war. Others were addicted to opium, amphetamines, and marijuana, all of which were cheap and easy to get.

Because Nixon chose to end the fighting gradually, anger and tension filled the land. Many young people hated their president, as they had Johnson before him. Julie told her father not to come to her graduation ceremony at Smith College. She feared that protesters would use his presence as an excuse to disrupt the ceremony. Nixon was heartbroken, but he reluctantly agreed.

At Kent State University, student protesters burned down the Reserve Officers' Training Corps (ROTC) building, and the National Guard moved in to restore order. Then, during an antiwar protest, the guardsmen started firing their guns. Four students were killed and eight were wounded—some were merely changing classes. In the investigation that followed, it became clear that the students had done nothing to threaten the guardsmen. The shootings sparked such an uproar that students at 450 colleges and universities went on strike. Many college presidents called on Nixon to end the war right away.

Nixon was concerned about the bad opinions that so many young people held of him. In the middle of one night, unable to sleep, he had his driver take him to the Lincoln Memorial, where he knew some students were gathering for a protest march the next day. The astonished students listened as Nixon rambled on about how they should travel the world and visit some of the places he had been. A few students tried to turn the conversation to Vietnam, but Nixon did not say much about it, except that he, too, wanted peace. The next day, hearing about the surprise visit, reporters rushed over to the Lincoln Memorial to interview the students. "I hope it was because he was tired," one girl said, "but most of what he was saying was absurd. Here we had come from a university that's uptight—on strike—and when we told him where we were from, he talked about the football team."

Although he was unpopular with many young people, Nixon was the president who signed the bill allowing them to vote at age eighteen instead of twenty-one. He was trying to move the country forward in other ways, too. Another of his innovative ideas, the Family Assistance Plan, grew out of his own experience of being poor as a young man. The plan would have drastically increased the amount of welfare aid given to working poor families. It would also have remedied the situation in which families were disqualified if the father lived at home but was unemployed or had a low-paying job. This system had led to fathers leaving home so that their families could receive welfare.

The plan passed in the House of Representatives, but it never even made it to the Senate floor for a vote. It was unpopular among Republican congressmen who thought it would cost too much money, while Democrats thought it didn't go far enough. Some critics said Nixon did not make enough of an effort to persuade the Senate to pass it because he was afraid it would make him too unpopular.

Nixon was a supporter of the Equal Rights Amendment, and he worked to reduce discrimination against women in government and in education. He created the Environmental Protection Agency to deal with smog and pollution. He established the Occupational Safety and Health Administration to make sure that employers were not forcing their workers to be in unsafe environments. He created a revenue-sharing plan in which the federal government returned six billion dollars a year to the states and cities for them to spend as they saw fit.

On civil rights, Nixon sent mixed messages. His Philadelphia Plan required construction unions, which had barred blacks from joining, to train black youths as apprentices and give them memberships as soon as they were qualified. But he did not favor busing students away from their neighborhoods in order to integrate schools. He asked the Southerners to form committees and come up with their own plans for desegregating the schools.

Although some people thought that was too lenient on Southern whites, the plan did require blacks and whites to serve side-by-side on the committees, which was a radical idea in itself. Once the Supreme Court declared that busing was legal, Nixon told the Justice Department

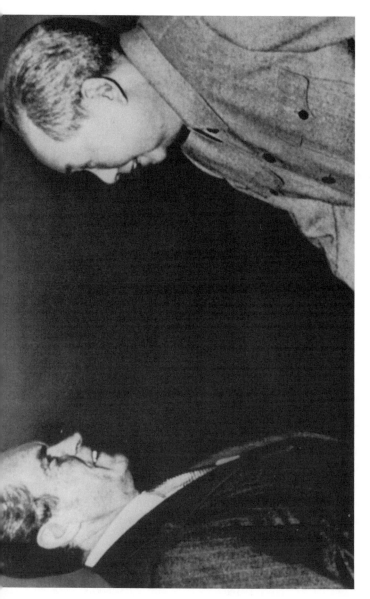

Nixon shaking the hand of Chairman Mao Tse-tung in 1972. His trip to China was one of Nixon's proudest foreign policy achievements.

to "Do what the law requires and not one bit more."

But Nixon was most interested in foreign policy. He believed that one nation the United States could not afford to ignore was The People's Republic of China. China, which had the greatest population of any nation in the world, had been closed to outsiders since the communists had taken it over in 1949. American and Chinese leaders had little contact in all of that time.

Nixon had come to realize that American-style government was simply not what all peoples of the world wanted. He saw China as a potential great power that the United States needed as an ally to keep the peace in Asia. In addition, relations were strained between China and the Soviet Union, which made it even more advantageous to befriend the Chinese. He believed in the old adage: "The enemy of my enemy is my friend." Also, Nixon hoped that the Chinese would encourage the North Vietnamese to end the war.

In 1954, Secretary of State John Foster Dulles had refused to shake the hand of Chou En-lai, the Chinese prime minister. Chou understandably had felt insulted. So it was a moving moment in 1972 as millions of Americans watched, on live television, as Nixon descended the steps of a plane, his hand outstretched to Chou. As the two men rode away from the airport in a curtained car, Chou said, "Your handshake came over the vastest ocean in the world—twenty-five years of no communication."

Chou took Nixon to meet Mao Tse-tung, chairman of the Communist Party. It was a sobering moment. Mao was a sickly old man, yet he was the most powerful leader of the most populated nation on Earth. He could snap his fingers, and his troops would kill thousands of people. Nixon talked to Mao for an hour, with the help of translators.

As they parted, Nixon told Mao that they both had something in common: Each had come from a poor family and risen to be a great leader of a powerful nation. To Nixon's delight, Mao replied, "Your book, *Six Crises,* is not a bad book."

During the rest of the week, Nixon toured legendary sites in China, including the Great Wall, which many Americans saw on television for the first time. Pat visited zoos, palaces, factories, and schools. As usual, she was a big hit everywhere she went.

At one of the banquets, Pat told Chou how much she loved seeing the giant pandas. "I'll give you some," Chou replied. In time, two giant pandas were delivered to the Washington National Zoo.

Another of Nixon's achievements was an agreement he reached with the Soviets to reduce the number of nuclear weapons—the Strategic Arms Limitation Treaty, or SALT. After months of secret negotiations by Kissinger, Nixon made a triumphant return to the country where he had held the famous "Kitchen Debates" with Kruschev years before.

Kruschev had fallen out of power, and Leonid Brezhnev was now the Soviet leader. Nixon met with him at the Royal Palace, and the two men discussed a variety of topics, including a joint orbit in space between Soviet and American astronauts, more trade, and cultural exchange.

Some people said that SALT gave the Soviets an advantage. Nixon, however, had achieved something no other president before him had been able to do. He had convinced the Soviets to agree to set limits on their destructive capability. The arms race had been spiraling out of control, with the United States and the Soviet Union each developing enough weapons to destroy the world many times over. It was a turning point in U.S.-Soviet relations.

In June 1972, Nixon announced that no new draftees would be sent to Vietnam. In October National Security Advisor Kissinger announced that "Peace was at hand" in the long war. It looked as though Nixon had finally kept his promise to end the war—but not a day too soon. He would be up for reelection in just a few months.

Nixon now had a reputation throughout the world as a peacemaker. But to those who worked most closely with him in the White House, Nixon had a very different image. He had become an angry, hostile man.

# Chapter Nine

## A Cancer Close to the Presidency

As the 1972 election year approached, Richard Nixon appeared to be unbeatable for reelection. His foreign policy achievements with the Soviet Union and China had earned him respect. His domestic policies were mostly popular, particularly his emphasis on law and order. And it seemed that he was finally finding a way to extract the United States from Vietnam.

But Nixon was worried. He never took elections for granted. He was convinced that his enemies were constantly scheming, and that most of the reporters resented his popularity with the American voters. He was convinced that they would stop at nothing to bring him down. Therefore, he would do what was necessary to assure victory in 1972.

One of the first things the Nixon campaign workers did was find a young man named Donald Segretti an office in California, far away from Washington, so that no one would know he was secretly working for the White House. Segretti found twenty-eight people in other states to help him wage what came to be called "dirty tricks" against Democratic opponents. They got letterhead stationery with Democratic candidates' names on it and wrote fake, embarrassing letters. Sometimes the letters manufactured stories the press would be interested in. Sometimes they wrote to a place where a candidate was scheduled to appear and said the candidate was cancelling the event. Segretti's goal was to embarrass and create havoc in opposing campaigns.

While the "Plumbers" group had been dissolved, several of the former "Plumbers," including G. Gordon Liddy and E. Howard Hunt, now worked for the Committee to Re-Elect the President, which came to be known as CREEP. The group's official task was to raise money for Nixon's reelection campaign, but CREEP members were up to some new espionage-type missions as well. On one mission in the early summer of 1972 five of them broke into the Democratic National Headquarters in the Watergate, an apartment and office building. Their mission was to plant listening devices, or "bugs," in order to eavesdrop and spy on the Democrats. They hoped to find out secret campaign strategies and embarrassing things that could be used against their candidate in the fall campaign.

The first "bugs" did not work. They decided to re-enter the Democratic headquarters. During the second break-in, on June 17, 1972, a security guard noticed something amiss and called the police. The officers arrived and arrested James McCord, who happened to be the security advisor for CREEP, and four Cuban refugees. The men were carrying walkie-talkies, canisters of Mace, electronic equipment, burglary tools, and fifty-three sequentially numbered $100 bills. To the police, it seemed like a routine break-in, until they discovered that one burglar was carrying an address book with the name "Howard Hunt" scrawled beside a phone number. When they dialed it, they discovered that it was to a phone in the White House.

When asked about the break-in over the next few days, Nixon's press secretary, Ron Ziegler, dismissed it as a third-rate burglary that had nothing to do with the White House. But secretly Nixon and his aides were very worried. If the CREEP connection to the burglars was made public, then all the illegal things the "Plumbers" had done, such as the break-in to Ellsberg's psychiatrist's office, would be revealed. This could seriously damage Nixon's chances for reelection.

Nixon ordered his assistants to go through files in the White House and destroy anything incriminating. In doing so, he went against his own better judgment. Eisenhower had once told Nixon, "Don't try to be cute or cover up. If you do, you will get so entangled you won't know what you're doing."

On June 23, 1972, Chief of Staff H.R. "Bob" Haldeman came into Nixon's office and told him some bad news. The FBI had traced the $100 bills found on the burglars straight to the Committee to Re-Elect the President. Haldeman said he thought he had a new way to solve the problem. The CIA was in charge of the FBI; Haldeman would call the director of the CIA and ask him to tell the FBI director to get off the Watergate case.

Nixon liked that idea. "Good deal," he said. "Play it tough. That's the way they play it and that's the way we are going to play it."

As he spoke, a hidden tape recorder was rolling. It was a voice-activated recorder that Nixon himself had installed. Other presidents— Eisenhower, Kennedy and Johnson—had recorded what went on in the Oval Office, too. Such recordings were invaluable to historians writing biographies of the presidents, and for the presidents themselves to use later when they wrote their own memoirs. Of course, only Haldeman and a few others knew that Nixon had a taping system, and Nixon assumed that its existence would remain secret.

In July 1972 the Democrats held their convention and nominated Senator George McGovern of South Dakota to run against Nixon. Nixon was delighted; he felt that McGovern would be easy to beat. He was right. The polls showed that he was far ahead.

As the campaign progressed, rumors about the Watergate break-in persisted, but they were overshadowed by good news from Vietnam. It appeared that the United States, South Vietnam, and North Vietnam were close to signing a formal peace agreement. National Security Advisor Kissinger told the press that "Peace was at hand." This good news carried Nixon into an overwhelming victory over McGovern. Nixon carried forty-nine states. It was a breathtaking triumph for a man who had barely won election four years before.

Instead of celebrating his victory, though, Nixon was subdued. Watergate was simmering in the back of his mind. He had also decided that many members of the White House staff and the cabinet were not doing a good job, and he was suspicious that some of them were leaking information or helping his "enemies." The morning after the election, Nixon called his entire cabinet to meet at the White House, where Haldeman asked for everyone's resignation.

On December 13, a little over a month after the election, the negotiations between the North and South Vietnamese broke off. To force the North Vietnamese back to the negotiating table, Nixon ordered more bombing. These raids quickly became known as the Christmas bombings and caused an uproar. Before the election, when he needed good news, Nixon had announced that a peace agreement was close. Now he was stepping up the war again. The stock market plummeted. Congressmen were furious; several publicly charged Nixon with lying to win an election.

Soon after Christmas, Nixon received word from the North Vietnamese that they would resume talks. On January 22, 1973, President Thieu of South Vietnam finally said he would sign the agreement, although he was very unhappy with the settlement. He had wanted all the communists to leave his country, but the agreement allowed 160,000 communist troops to stay there. It even called for communists to hold some offices in his government. Although Nixon tried to put a good face on the settlement, it was obvious that, after all the lives that had been lost, the South Vietnamese and Americans had fallen far short of a victory.

Meanwhile, the cover-up of the Watergate break-in was unraveling. On March 21, 1973, presidential counsel John Dean came to see Nixon. Watergate was a serious problem, Dean said. "We have a cancer— within, close to the presidency, that's growing. It's growing daily."

Dean told Nixon that G. Gordon Liddy, E. Howard Hunt, and others had said they would remain quiet only if they received money, and that $350,000 had been paid out of Haldeman's White House safe. To Dean's astonishment, Nixon didn't seem surprised. Dean realized he must have already known about the payoffs.

"There's going to be a continual blackmail operation by Hunt and Liddy and the Cubans," Dean told Nixon. Hunt wanted another $120,000, he said.

"How much money do you need?" Nixon asked.

"I would say these people are going to cost a million dollars over the next two years," Dean replied.

"We could get that," Nixon said. "You could get a million dollars. You could get it in cash. I know where it could be gotten."

Meanwhile, hidden away, the tape recorder was running.

Dean said there was another problem. Hunt and Liddy and the others would also expect Nixon, as president, to pardon them so they would not go to prison. If Nixon did that, he would look guilty as well.

"No, it's wrong, that's for sure," Nixon said. Months later, there would be intense debate over what he meant by that statement. Nixon would claim he was saying it would be wrong to pardon Hunt and Liddy. Others would say that he only meant he could not get away with it.

By now, Judge John Sirica, who was hearing the case against the burglars, had grown suspicious that there was more to the Watergate break-in than a bungled burglary. He sentenced Hunt to thirty-five years in prison and the Cuban burglars to forty years each. He also announced from the bench that he would reduce their sentences if they cooperated with investigators. Sirica's tough action worked. One of the men, James McCord, handed Sirica a note saying he feared for his life, that he wanted to cooperate.

Meanwhile, Dean was beginning to fear, correctly, that Nixon, Haldeman, and Ehrlichman were going to pin the blame for Watergate on him. He, too, decided to cooperate with the prosecutors.

Nixon, apparently suspecting that Dean was going to cooperate with his enemies, called Dean into his office. He asked Dean if he remembered when the "cancer close to the presidency" discussion took place. "That's when you brought the facts in to me for the first time, isn't it? And gave me the whole picture?" Nixon asked.

Dean thought this was an odd question, and the president seemed to be behaving strangely. He also felt that Nixon was lying. Then, Nixon said, "You know, that mention I made to you about a million dollars and so forth as no problem . . . I was just joking, of course, when I said that."

Then, Nixon took Dean to another corner of the room and continued the conversation, this time in a lower voice. For the first time, Dean began to suspect that there might be a tape recorder running. A few days later, he resigned.

Now Nixon realized that in order to save himself and his presidency, he would have to pin the blame for Watergate on Ehrlichman and Haldeman. He summoned them to Camp David, where he called each man in, one at a time, and tearfully told them the bad news. He wanted them to resign.

At a press conference, Nixon said that Haldeman and Ehrlichman were "two of the finest public servants it has been my privilege to know." He said he did not want to take the easy way out by blaming these men for his troubles. Yet, minutes later, he added, "I will do everything in my power to ensure that the guilty are brought to justice." But, he was not one of the guilty. He insisted that he had known nothing about the break-in and cover-up until many months after it happened.

Nixon was lonely without Haldeman and Ehrlichman. He never trusted the men who took their place the same way. He told the lawyers who had been hired to defend him that he had not been involved in the cover-up. He insisted that he knew nothing about money that was paid to the burglars, or about the attempts to call the FBI off the case.

His lawyers, however, were denied access to any of his papers— even the notes that had been written by Haldeman, Ehrlichman, and others. "I am not going to allow anybody to look at those papers," Nixon said. "You understand? *They're mine.*" To Alexander Haig, who took Haldeman's place, Nixon said, "Believe me, I knew nothing about it (Watergate), no Goddamn thing."

One loyal friend was Nixon's secretary, Rose Mary Woods. Seeing how distressed Nixon was by the increasing pressure of congressional hearings and criminal investigations, and believing he was innocent, she felt sorry for her boss. "You'd be surprised how many people say, 'you know, God does bring the hardest problems to the strongest men,'" she told him. "I'm just praying that God has given you enough strength to take this."

Meanwhile, Vice President Agnew was in trouble of his own. He was being investigated for taking bribes when he had been governor of Maryland. Donald Segretti, who had run the "dirty tricks" campaign, had been caught, too. As more men who had been associated with the "Plumbers" were arrested, all of their illegal deeds came to light. The attorney general of the United States, who was appointed by Nixon, finally gave in to the public pressure and appointed a special prosecutor, Archibald Cox, to delve further into Watergate. One of the chief questions for Cox to answer was how involved in the entire scandal was the president of the United States.

To Nixon, everything seemed to be unraveling. To make matters worse, the North Vietnamese were violating the peace settlement.

The Senate established a committee to investigate Watergate. Senator Sam Ervin of North Carolina was named the chairman. During the summer of 1973 the committee's hearings were televised. Every day, millions of Americans watched the case against Nixon and his men unfold.

Nixon knew that John Dean was scheduled to go on television to testify against him. As that day approached, he considered what he might do to distract the American people from the hearings. He decided to prove, once and for all, that other presidents had done illegal things, too—that former Presidents Johnson and Kennedy in particular had allowed, even encouraged, the FBI and the Secret Service to tap their enemies' phones. As usual, Nixon felt that reporters were out to get him while they had ignored what Johnson and Kennedy had done.

"I don't want all this Goddamned hypocrisy," Nixon roared to Henry Kissinger, his national security advisor. "Well, if we can get the names (of those who had been tapped by the former presidents), Mr. President, we ought to put some of them out," Kissinger replied. "Not some—all of them, Nixon snarled. "I'm going to put the whole damn . . . list out."

In June 1973, Dean testified that Nixon knew about the break-in far sooner than he claimed. But even more fascinating was the atmosphere Dean described in the White House—the hostility, the paranoia, the list of Nixon's perceived enemies.

At this point it was still Dean's word against the president's. Who was telling the truth? The taping system was still a secret. Nixon seemed to be safe.

Then an aide, Alexander Butterfield, who had worked for Haldeman in the past, testified before the Senate committee. One of the men questioning him was a former FBI agent named Donald Sanders. Sanders had been intrigued by something Dean had said in his testimony. Dean mentioned that he believed he had been taped during his conversations in the Oval Office. Sanders asked Butterfield if he knew of any

John Ehrlichman, Nixon's domestic policy advisor, was forced to resign because of the Watergate cover-up.

H.R. (Bob) Haldeman, another casualty of the Watergate scandal, was Nixon's closest aide.

reason why Nixon would have taken Dean to another corner of the room and spoken to him quietly.

"I was hoping you fellows would ask me that," Butterfield answered. "I've wondered what I would say. I'm concerned about the effect my answer will have on national security and international affairs.... Well, yes, there's a recording system in the White House."

Sanders and the others listened as Butterfield explained how the system worked. A few days later, Butterfield told his story to the entire Senate committee on live television.

Most Americans could not believe that Nixon was taping all of his conversations. Even Pat did not know she was being taped. Everyone who had visited the Oval Office racked their brains, trying to remember what they had said during their visits. Many expressed outrage at being secretly recorded.

Some of Nixon's aides told him he should burn the tapes right away. If he waited, the Senate committee or Judge Sirica could issue a subpoena for them, and Nixon would be violating the law if he did not turn them over. After all, they said, the tapes were his personal property to do with as he wished.

But Nixon decided it would make him look terribly guilty to burn the tapes. And, as long as he could pick and choose what people heard, the tapes might actually help his case.

It didn't take long for the subpoenas for the tapes to come. Nixon refused to turn over the tapes. He said that the tapes had captured his conversations about sensitive issues that would threaten national security if released to the public. Instead, he would have his secretary, Rose Mary Woods, transcribe the tapes, and he would release the written record. To assure everyone that he was being honest, he would ask an impartial observer, Senator John Stennis, to verify that they were accurate. This suggestion was ridiculed because Senator Stennis was seventy-two years old and nearly deaf.

In October 1973, Syria and Egypt attacked Israel. The Middle East again erupted in war. Henry Kissinger went to the area to negotiate a settlement. Although Nixon was back in Washington, telling Kissinger what to say, Kissinger got all the credit when an agreement was reached.

The same month, the prosecutors investigating Vice President Agnew told Nixon that they had never seen such overwhelming evidence against a person. Agnew had no choice but to resign from the vice presidency. Nixon appointed Congressman Gerald R. Ford to take his place.

Then, one Saturday night in October 1973, Special Prosecutor Archibald Cox announced that he would refuse to accept written transcripts. He wanted the actual tapes. Nixon refused to back down. He called Attorney General Elliot Richardson and told him to fire Cox. Richardson said he would rather resign, and he did just that. Nixon then called the deputy attorney general, who said he would resign, too, rather than fire Cox. Finally, Nixon found the next person in line for the job of attorney general. He was Solicitor General Robert Bork. Bork agreed to fire Cox. Next, in an effort to make sure that no one else could be appointed special prosecutor, Nixon dissolved the entire job. His goal was to be free of the special prosecutor.

This "Saturday Night Massacre," as it came to be called, created a huge media backlash against Nixon. Senator Edmund Muskie said that Nixon's behavior "smacks of dictatorship." One newspaper columnist asked, "Has President Nixon gone crazy?"

Nixon had entered office with great plans for America—welfare reform, national health insurance, more loans for college students—plus an end to the Vietnam War that he thought would not weaken international respect for the United States. But by the second year of his second term in office, the Watergate problem consumed his every waking moment. People invited to the White House for dinner with Nixon and his family began noticing mood swings. There were rumors that he was drinking too much, but others who knew him well, including Haldeman and his daughter Julie, said Nixon did not have a problem with alcohol.

Reporters continued to hound him about Watergate as well as about his personal finances. It was reported that he owed back income taxes. One day, as he faced reporters, sweat beading on his brow, Nixon scowled and said, "I welcome this kind of examination, because people have got to know whether or not their president is a crook. Well, I am not a crook. I have earned everything I have got."

This line became fodder for the stand-up comedians. It became clear that few people believed the statement. When the news broke that one of the subpoenaed Oval Office tapes had an eighteen-and-one-half-minute gap, investigators examined the tapes and said that someone had deliberately erased the section. Rose Mary Woods said it was her fault, that she accidentally erased part of a tape when she stopped transcribing to take a phone call. The famous eighteen-and-a-half-minute gap also became a favorite subject for comedians.

The House of Representatives began discussing impeaching Richard Nixon. This meant they would vote to have him tried in the Senate for "high crimes and misdemeanors." If they succeeded, Nixon would be only the second president in history to be impeached. The first had been President Andrew Johnson, 105 years before.

He agonized over whether he should end the agony by resigning. But every time he brought it up, Pat, Tricia- and her husband, Ed Cox, and Julie and David talked him out of it. He had to stay in for the good of the country, they said. He had to fight back.

The cancer on the presidency was growing, just as Dean had predicted. Haldeman, Ehrlichman and several others were facing trials for several crimes. Their lawyers wanted the tapes, too. And the Internal Revenue Service announced that Nixon had taken some illegal deductions on his income taxes and owed the federal government an additional $432,787.

Throughout the spring and summer of 1974, Nixon continued to refuse to turn over the tapes. Again, he had Rose Woods and fifteen other secretaries start transcribing them. Then Nixon looked over what they had typed. He was bothered by all the curse words that he had said. Every time he saw one, he crossed it out and wrote "expletive deleted" in its place. "If my mother ever heard me use words like that, she would turn over in her grave," Nixon said.

Nixon made a television appearance. Sitting beside a stack of bound copies of the transcripts, he assured the viewers that the entire truth of Watergate was included in the volumes. He hoped this would put an end to the calls for the tapes.

It didn't work. One of the problems with the transcripts was the high number of "expletive deleted" cuts. Most of the words Nixon crossed out were "damn" and "hell." But when the public read portions of the transcripts in the newspapers, they assumed he had said much worse. The term "expletive deleted" became another big joke. But even more appalling was the anger and hostility that came through in the transcripts. Americans were shocked that the president of the United States could be so mean-spirited.

Nixon decided to let the Supreme Court decide whether he had to turn over the tapes. In the meantime, he went to the Middle East to talk about the peace process with the leaders there. Through the whole trip, he suffered from phlebitis, a painful swelling of a vein, in one of his legs. He ignored his doctor's warning to stay off his leg. As he rode through the Nile River Delta in Egypt, six million people gathered along the route, all of them cheering for President Nixon. It was an incredible moment, but it was also a sad one for Nixon. He knew, deep down, that even though people of other nations viewed him as one of the great peacemakers of his time, Watergate would force him out of the White House, one way or the other.

On July 24, 1974, the Supreme Court ruled Nixon would have to turn over the tapes. It was a moment of reckoning. He had told everyone—his family, his friends in the House and the Senate, and the American people—that he had not been involved in covering up Watergate. Now everyone was going to hear the tape recording of his June 23, 1972, conversation with Haldeman, when the president and his top aide talked about the burglary just six days after it happened, and how they planned to ask the CIA to order the FBI off the case.

Meanwhile, the House Judiciary Committee met and approved three Articles of Impeachment. Article I said that Nixon had known about the Watergate burglary and obstructed justice by trying to cover it up. Article II said that Nixon had abused the powers of the presidency with the "Plumbers," wiretapping, and misusing the CIA and FBI. Article III said that Nixon tried to hinder the impeachment process by refusing to turn over tapes. Now the entire House of Representatives would vote on the articles. Several Republicans on the committee voted for impeachment. Nixon's base of support was crumbling.

The only way to end this humiliation was by resigning. But Nixon decided to wait a few more days. He would release the June 23, 1972, tape, then wait for the reaction. If he had even a small group of supporters left in the House of Representatives, there would not be enough votes for impeachment.

The tape was released, and the reaction was devastating. Ten Republicans on the Judiciary Committee who had voted against the articles of impeachment said they now wanted Nixon to resign. Vice President Ford, who had said he did not think Nixon deserved impeachment, now told Nixon that, had he known what was on that tape, he never would have made those statements.

Senator Barry Goldwater called Alexander Haig, Nixon's new chief of staff, and relayed a message: "Al, Dick Nixon has lied to me for the very last time. And to a hell of a lot of others in the Senate and House. We're sick to death of it all."

Finally, after all these months of denying everything, Nixon decided he must resign. He sat up until 2 a.m. in the Lincoln Sitting Room working on his resignation speech. When he finally went to bed, he found a note from Julie lying on his pillow. "Dear Daddy—I love you. Whatever you do I will support. I am very proud of you. Please wait a week or even ten days before you make this decision. Go through the fire just a little bit longer. You are so strong! I love you, Julie." At the bottom, she had added: "Millions support you."

If anything could have changed Nixon's mind, it would have been Julie's note. But it was too late. Deep down in his heart, he knew that resigning would be the best thing for the country.

The next day, Nixon told Kissinger, who was now the secretary of state, of his decision and asked him to notify foreign governments. Kissinger was touched by Nixon's sadness. He put his arm around Nixon and said, "History will treat you more kindly than your contemporaries have."

Nixon went back to the residence part of the White House where his family was already packing their things. Nixon asked a photographer to come in to take their picture, the last one they would have made in the White House. Pat protested. No one wanted to have their picture taken right now, she said. But Nixon insisted. It was "for history," he

Nixon, Pat, and daughter Julie, as he announces his resignation from the presidency, August 8, 1974.

said. They stood together, smiling through their tears, as the flash went off. Julie sobbed and threw her arms around her father. The photographer captured that moment, too.

As Nixon faced the television cameras the night of August 8, 1974, 110 million people watched and another forty million listened on the radio. It was a talk no American had ever heard from a president before: "Because of the Watergate matter, I might not have the support of the Congress that I would consider necessary to make the very difficult decisions and carry out the duties of this office in the way the interests of the nation will require. . . . Therefore, I shall resign the presidency effective at noon tomorrow."

He continued, "I regret deeply any injuries that may have been done in the course of the events that led to this decision. I would say only that if some of my judgments were wrong—and some were very wrong— they were made in what I believed at the time to be the best interest of the nation."

The next day, after sentimental good-byes to his closest associates, and to the people who worked in the White House—the people who had cleaned the rooms and cooked their meals—the Nixons walked down a long, scarlet carpet to the South Lawn, where an olive green Marine helicopter waited to take them away.

As he prepared to board the helicopter, Nixon paused, turned and shook Ford's hand. "Good-bye, Mr. President," he said to Ford, who would be sworn in as president in just a few hours.

As he reached the top of the helicopter's steps, Richard Nixon turned to face the cameras. He lifted both arms and spread his fingers into a "V-for-Victory" sign and broke into a huge smile.

The helicopter flew the Nixons to St. Andrews Air Force base where Air Force One was waiting to fly him home to California. As the plane flew over Missouri, new President Gerald Ford gave his inauguration address. Nixon was not listening, so he did not hear Ford's first sentence:

"Our long national nightmare is over."

# Chapter Ten

## The Elder Statesman

One of the unchecked powers of the presidency is the ability to pardon people accused of crimes. Gerald Ford, the nation's new president, was now faced with the first big decision of his term in office: whether to pardon Richard Nixon.

Ford eventually decided that Nixon should be pardoned—not so much for his own good, but for the good of the country. If Nixon were not pardoned, he would almost certainly face criminal charges. It could be as long as a year before the case went to trial. It would be nearly impossible to find twelve impartial, unbiased people to serve on the jury. Watergate had already been an American obsession for two years, and a Nixon trial would drag it out many more months. It would be degrading for the United States to have an ex-president being tried on national television. Ford felt that the nation needed to move forward, that the wounds needed to heal.

Ford had one request: He wanted Nixon to admit that he had actively participated in the cover-up. Nixon refused. He agreed only to say that he had been preoccupied with running the country and had made a mistake by turning so many decisions over to men like Dean, Haldeman, and Ehrlichman. Ford sent a lawyer on the White House staff, Benton Becker, to California to try to reason with Nixon.

Becker entered Nixon's small office at his California home and was shocked to see how terrible Nixon looked. "He appeared to have aged and shrunken . . . since his resignation," Becker reported to Ford. "His jowls were loose and flabby, and his shirt seemed to be too big for his neck . . . His handshake was very weak." Becker and Nixon spoke for twenty minutes, with Becker doing most of the talking. Finally, he gave up. On his way out, however, he was summoned back to Nixon's office.

"You've been a fine young man," Nixon said. "You've been a gentleman. We've had enough bullies. I want to give you something. But look around the office. I don't have anything any more. They took it all away from me."

"That's all right, Mr. President," Becker said awkwardly.

"No, no, no," Nixon said. "I asked Pat to get these for me. She got these out of my own jewelry box." He took out two little boxes containing cuff links and a tiepin. "There aren't any more in the whole world. I want you to have them."

When he got back to Washington, Becker told Ford that he believed Nixon would not live much longer. Years later, he said he feared Nixon would commit suicide.

Nixon may have been depressed and sickly, but he still had his pride. He would not admit to anything further. On September 8, Ford went on national television to say he was granting Nixon a pardon. Then Nixon released his statement: "I was wrong in not acting more decisively and more forthrightly in dealing with Watergate, particularly when it reached the state of judicial proceedings and grew from a political scandal into a national tragedy. No words can describe the depths of my regret and pain at the anguish my mistakes over Watergate have caused the nation and the Presidency—a nation I so deeply love and an institution I so greatly respect."

At the time, most Americans were outraged that Ford pardoned Nixon. Some accused Ford of striking a deal with Nixon before he resigned: that Nixon would hand over the presidency to Ford in exchange for a pardon. At any rate, the pardon may have been part of the reason why Ford lost the 1976 election to former Georgia governor Jimmy Carter. Now, years later, many of the critics have changed their minds and believe that Ford did the right thing. The country could not have stood to be torn apart by Richard Nixon and the Watergate scandal any longer.

The pardon did not solve the question of what would be done with all the thousands of hours of tapes and the millions of documents that piled up in the White House during Nixon's presidency. Before Nixon, presidents had been allowed to take these things as their personal property. In Nixon's case, the government was still prosecuting many of those involved in Watergate and wanted the tapes and papers as evidence. Congress passed the Presidential Records and Materials Preservation Act of 1974, which gave control of the materials to the National Archives, where they were kept sealed in a vault. Nixon was allowed to look at them, but he could not take them out of the building.

Nixon's phlebitis continued to be a problem, and he finally, in October 1974, had to have surgery on a clot in his leg. The surgery went well, but a few hours later, Nixon slipped into a coma. For a while, it looked as though he might not survive. But, with his usual determination, he fought his way back to health.

He was rarely seen for the first couple of years after his resignation, but by 1976, Nixon was ready to begin yet another comeback. This time the battle would not be for a political office, but for his reputation, for his place in history.

He went back to China to visit Mao Tse-Tung and other new leaders of the Chinese government. Chou En-lai had died. Nixon's return to China—the first of several trips he would make before his death—dominated the front pages of newspapers for days. Many criticized him for going, saying it was an embarrassment to the United States.

There were other controversies. Bob Woodward and Carl Bernstein, two *Washington Post* reporters who had gained fame for their investigation of the Watergate scandal, published *The Final Days,* a book about Nixon's last months in office. The book portrayed Nixon as an unstable man who drank heavily and wandered around the White House talking to portraits on the walls. The book's version of the climactic meeting between Kissinger and Nixon, after the decision to resign had been made, had them falling to their knees to pray. Kissinger said Woodward and Bernstein grossly distorted what happened. At the same time, a movie came out based on Woodward and Bernstein's first book, *All the President's Men,* about the Watergate scandal. The next year,

British broadcaster David Frost paid Nixon $600,000 for the privilege of doing a series of interviews with him. Clearly, the American people were still fascinated by Richard Nixon.

As he grew older, Nixon mellowed. He seemed to have less anger toward those he perceived as enemies. Pat suffered a stroke in 1976, and he spent many hours by her bedside, reading her a few of the one million letters that poured in from well-wishers everywhere. The illness was difficult for Pat. In all her life she had rarely been sick. Learning to use her hands again, even climbing three steps in physical therapy, proved agonizingly difficult. She had been everyone's rock during all of Nixon's turmoils—the fund crisis and the Checkers speech, the heartbreaking election losses, the Watergate scandal. Her son-in-law David said, "She is a shoulder to everyone—but whose shoulder does she lean on?" Now she had to learn how to lean on her husband. He fussed over Julie and Tricia as well, worrying whether they were eating enough and getting enough rest. He spent more time doting on his grandchildren than he had with his own daughters. He and Pat eventually moved to New York to be closer to Tricia, her husband, Ed Cox, and their family.

Slowly but surely, Nixon regained respectability. He flew to Kentucky to dedicate a recreation center that had been built with money from his revenue-sharing program. He wrote his memoirs, then proceeded to write eight more books about foreign policy and the great world leaders he had met. He was a guest on the *Today* show every day for a week in 1980, commenting on the presidential race between Jimmy Carter and Ronald Reagan.

He also seemed more willing to admit his mistakes, and to face his old enemies, the reporters. As a guest on *Meet the Press,* Nixon said that, if he had bombed the North Vietnamese much sooner, he could have ended the war in 1969 rather than 1973. "That was the biggest mistake of my presidency."

On Watergate, he said, "It was a small thing, the break-in, and break-ins have occurred previously in other campaigns as well. At that point, we should have done something about it. We should have exposed it, found out who did it, rather than attempting to contain it, to cover it up.

It was the cover-up that was wrong, and that was a very big thing; there's no question about it at all."

In 1990, Nixon spoke at the opening of the Richard Nixon Library and Birthplace in his hometown of Yorba Linda, California. The library was more like a museum and gift shop compared to the ones other former presidents had opened because it contained few documents; they were all still sealed in the National Archives. Nevertheless, the ceremony brought out President George Bush and former presidents Ronald Reagan and Gerald Ford, along with their wives. Pat made her first public appearance in ten years. In fact, during their presidencies, Reagan, Ford, and Bush sometimes called Nixon on the telephone or met with him in person to seek his advice, particularly on foreign policy. After President Bill Clinton was elected in 1992, he also occasionally asked for Nixon's help.

In 1993, just one day after her fifty-third wedding anniversary, Pat Nixon died of lung cancer. Nixon had lost his closest friend and partner. He wept openly at her funeral. She was laid to rest on the grounds at the Nixon Library.

Less than a year later, Richard Nixon suffered a stroke and slipped into a coma. He never regained consciousness. On April 22, 1994, Richard Nixon passed away. Forty-two thousand people passed by his coffin at the Nixon Library to pay their last respects.

Once again, Reagan, Ford and Bush, this time joined by former President Jimmy Carter, gathered for Nixon's funeral at the Nixon Library and Birthplace. As President Clinton got up to speak, he looked over at the little house Richard Nixon had been born in, a house that Frank Nixon had built with his own sweat.

"From these humble roots, as from so many humble beginnings in this country, grew the force of a driving dream," Clinton said. There were some familiar old faces sitting there, listening—former Vice President Spiro Agnew, who had resigned in disgrace, G. Gordon Liddy, one of the "Plumbers," and Elliot Richardson, who had resigned in the "Saturday Night Massacre."

Many remarked on how odd it was that he had risen from such humiliation in 1974 to such words of praise twenty years later. But anyone who had followed the peaks and valleys of his career should not have been surprised.

Even in death, disturbing news about Nixon continues to come forth. In 1996, the National Archives began releasing 3,700 hours of tapes never heard before by the public. The tapes show the darkest side of Nixon. Even before the Watergate break-in and cover-up engulfed his presidency, he seemed to have been a suspicious man who used vulgar language and profanity frequently.

On one tape, Nixon complains that the Internal Revenue Service has harrassed several of his friends, even evangelist Billy Graham, about their contributions to his presidential campaign. Full of rage, Nixon orders Haldeman to retaliate by asking the IRS to investigate the big contributors to the Democratic Party, too. "Bob, please get me the names of the Jews, you know, the big Jewish contributors of the Democrats," He is also heard making negative comments about blacks and women on some tapes.

On another tape, made just two weeks after the Watergate break-in, Nixon is heard suggesting that his men wreck the Republican National Headquarters to make it look as though a break-in had occurred there, too.

Nixon will always be one of the least understood presidents. Why did he cover up Watergate? Why did he tape himself? What caused him to be so suspicious, so secretive, so hostile? Did his family teach him not to let anyone be close to him, not to trust anyone?

Bryce Harlow, one of his former associates, said, "I suspect that my gifted friend somewhere in his youth, maybe when he was very young or in his teens, got badly hurt by someone he cared for very deeply or trusted totally—a parent, a relative, a dear friend, a lover, a confidante. Somewhere I figure somebody hurt him badly, and from that experience and from then on he could not trust people."

Perhaps Nixon shed the most light on these questions by something he said just after he resigned from office. "What starts the process, really, are the laughs and snubs and slights you get when you are a kid," he said. "Sometimes it's because you're poor or Irish or Jewish or ugly or simply that you are skinny. But if you're reasonably intelligent and if

Richard Nixon lived for twenty years after resigning the presidency. Over the years his political advice became more highly valued. Here he comments on the 1988 presidential race on a national news show.

your anger is deep enough and strong enough, you learn that you can change those attitudes by excellence, personal gut performance, while those who have everything are sitting on their fat butts."

Once you get to the top, Nixon added, "You find you can't stop playing the game the way you've always played it because it is a part of you and you need it as much as you do an arm or a leg. So you are lean and mean and resourceful, and you continue to walk on the edge of the precipice because over the years you have become fascinated by how close to the edge you can walk without losing your balance."

From now on, students of history will read that Nixon was the first president ever to reach a nuclear arms treaty with the Soviet Union. He reopened China to the world. He pulled the United States out of Vietnam. He had hopes that were ahead of his time—health insurance for all, more college loans for students.

He also broke the law and was forced out of office in disgrace. He was one of the first candidates ever to use negative campaigning, which is commonplace today. After Watergate, the press gained more power and became more aggressive in how it covered our leaders. Most importantly, many Americans never trusted politicians again. Richard Nixon may have influenced American politics in the second half of the twentieth century more than any other politician.

More than anything else, Richard Nixon wanted to make his mark on history. For better and for worse, he did.

# Timeline

1913  Richard Milhous Nixon born in Yorba Linda, California.

1934  graduates from Whittier College.

1937  graduates from Duke University Law School.

1940  marries Pat Ryan.

1942  joins the U.S. Navy.

1946  wins election to the U.S. House of Representatives.

1950  elected to the U.S. Senate.

1952  elected vice-president of the United States.

1960  loses race for the presidency to John F. Kennedy.

1962  loses a race for governor of California. Gives his "last press conference."

1968  elected President of the United States.

1972  relected president by the biggest landslide ever.

1974  resigns the presidency after the cover-up of the Watergate break-in unravels.

1993  Pat Nixon dies.

1994  Richard Nixon dies and is buried at the Nixon Library and Birthplace in Yorba Linda, California.

# Bibliography

**Books**

Ambrose, Stephen E., *Eisenhower: The President*, Vol. II. New York: Simon and Schuster, 1984.

———, Nixon: *The Education of a Politician, 1913-1962*, Vol. I. New York: Simon and Schuster, 1987.

———, *Nixon: Ruin and Recovery, 1973-1990*, Vol. III. New York: Simon and Schuster, 1991.

———, *Nixon: The Triumph of a Politician, 1962-1972*, Vol. II. New York: Simon and Schuster, 1989.

Brodie, Fawn, *Richard Nixon: The Shaping of His Character*. New York: W.W. Norton & Company, 1981.

de Toledano, Ralph, *One Man Alone: Richard Nixon*. New York: Funk & Wagnalls, 1969.

Dean, John, *Blind Ambition: The White House Years*. New York: Simon and Schuster, 1976.

Drew, Elizabeth, *Washington Journal*. New York: Random House, 1975.

Eisenhower, Julie Nixon, *Pat Nixon: The Untold Story*. New York: Kensington Publishing Corp., 1986.

Ford, Gerald R., *A Time to Heal: The Autobiography of Gerald Ford*. New York, Harper & Row, 1979.

Hadleman, H.R., *The Ends of Power*. New York: The New York Times Book Company, Inc., 1978.

Kornitzer, Bela, *The Real Nixon: An Intimate Biography*. Chicago: Rand McNally, 1960.

Kutler, Stanley I, ed., *Abuse of Power: The New Nixon Tapes*. New York: Simon and Schuster, 1997.

Mazo, Earl, *Richard Nixon: A Political and Personal Portrait*. New
    York: Harper & Brothers, 1959.
Nixon, Richard, *RN: The Memoirs of Richard Nixon*. New York:
    Grosset & Dunlap, 1978.
————, *Six Crises*. Garden City, N.Y.: Doubleday & Company, 1962.
Safire, William, *Before the Fall: An Inside View of the Pre-Watergate
    White House*. Garden City, N.Y.: Doubleday & Company,
1975.
Thompson, Kenneth W., *The Nixon Presidency*. New York: The
    University Press of America, 1987.

**Periodicals**
*Good Housekeeping*, June 1960.

*Los Angeles Times*, November 6, 1962.

*New York Times*, February 4, 1968.
————July 19, 1968.
————January 21, 1969.
————March 31, 1969.
————September 9, 1974.
————April 11, 1988.

*Washington Post*, August 9, 1979.

# Sources

CHAPTER ONE
*The Last Press Conference*
**10** "As I leave you. . . ." "California: Career's End," *Time,* November 16 1962,
p. 28
**10** "To the great majority of my supporters..." Nixon, Richard. *RN:
The Memoirs of Richard Nixon.* New York: Grosset & Dunlap, 1978,
p. 246.

CHAPTER TWO
*The Early Years*
**12** "Naturally we then began to quarrel. . ." Kornitzer, Bela. *The Real
Nixon: An Intimate Biography.* Chicago: Rand McNally,
1960, p. 62.
**12** "Do you like water?" Ambrose, Stephen E. *Nixon: The Education of
a Politician, 1913-1962,* Vol. I. New York: Simon and Schuster, 1987,
p. 23.
**12** "...but she would just sit you down. . ." ibid., p. 24.
**12** "...I'll be a lawyer they can't bribe." de Toledano, Ralph. *One Man Alone:
Richard Nixon.* New York: Funk & Wagnalls, 1969, p. 26
**13** "Like any twelve-year-old I was happy to see them..." Nixon, op.cit.,
p. 9.
**13** "He put his arms around her and said that he wanted to pray ..." ibid.,
p. 11.
**16** "It was during Harold's long illness that my mother..." ibid., p. 11.
**18** "He barely had the strength to walk..." ibid., p. 12.
**18** "sank into a deep, impenetrable silence." Schreiber, R. "Richard Nixon:
A Mother's Story," *Good Housekeeping,* June 1960, p. 212.
**18** "He inspired in us. . ." Nixon, op.cit., p. 19-20.
**20** "I'll manage all right. . ." Brodie, Fawn. *Richard Nixon: The Shaping of
His Character.* New York: W.W. Norton & Company, 1981, p. 125.
**23** "I'd like to have a date with you." Ambrose, op.cit., p. 93.

CHAPTER THREE
*Tricky Dick*
**34** "Richard, why don't you drop the case?.." Schreiber, op.cit., p. 214.
**34** "The ass under the lion's skin is Crosley." Ambrose, op.cit., p. 182.
**36** "I'm sorry about that episode. . ." *New Republic,* May 5, 1958.

CHAPTER FOUR
*A Dog Named Checkers*
**38** "I'm glad you are going to be on the team, Dick." Nixon, op.cit., p. 87.
**40** "There has just been a meeting. . ." ibid., p. 102.
**42** "I don't think I can go through with this one," ibid., p. 103.
**42** "My fellow Americans. . ." Mazo, Earl. *Richard Nixon: A Political and Personal Portrait.* New York: Harper & Brothers, 1959, p. 129-131.
**45** "General, you didn't need to come out to the airport," Nixon, op.cit., p. 106.
**45** "In politics, most people are your friends only as long. . ." ibid., p. 110.

CHAPTER FIVE
*Second in Command*
**47** "Here's my last campaign speech, Murray," Nixon, op.cit., p. 163.
**47** "You get back there, Dick..." Nixon, op.cit., p. 176.
**49** "You do all the talking. . ." Ambrose, op.cit., p. 524.
**50** "This time we bought our own flowers!" Nixon, Richard. *Six Crises.* Garden City, N.Y.: Doubleday, 1962, p. 283-285.

CHAPTER SIX
*Two Heartbreaking Losses*
**54** "If you give me a week, I might think of one. " Ambrose, Stephen E. *Eisenhower: The President,* Vol. II. New York: Simon & Schuster, 1984, p. 604.
**56** "No, no, don't concede!" Ambrose, *Nixon,* Vol. I, p. 605.
**59** "...I will support your decision." Nixon, op.cit., p. 240.
**59** "When I become *President...*" *Los Angeles Times,* November 6, 1962.

CHAPTER SEVEN
*Victory Out of Chaos*
**61** "... I had what every politician dreads most. . ." Nixon, op.cit., p. 266.
**62** "Richard, don't *you* give up..." ibid., p. 288.
**64** "When the strongest nation. . ." *New York Times,* February 4, 1968.
**66** "Dick, I don't want there to be any more question. . ." Nixon, op.cit., p. 307.
**66** " ... and above all, his integrity." *New York Times,* July 19, 1968.

**68** "And I say let's win this one for Ike." ibid., August 9, 1968.

**69** "Having lost a close one eight years ago ..." Nixon, op.cit., p. 335.

**69** "Four more years of death!" *New York Times,* January 21, 1969.

## CHAPTER EIGHT
### *President Nixon*

**70** "..one of the giants of our time," *New York Times,* March 31, 1969.

**71** "It shows you're a weakling, Mr. President." Haldeman, H.R.*The Ends of Power.* New York: The New York Times Book Company, Inc., 1978, p. 110.

**71** "I want you to set up a little group..." ibid., p. 112.

**72** "You talk to Hunt. I want the break-in," Kutler, Stanley I., *Abuse of Power: The New Nixon Tapes.* New York: Simon & Schuster, 1997, p. 6.

**72** "Get someone to hit him ..." Ambrose, Stephen E., *Nixon: The Triumph of a Politician 1962-1972,* Vol. II. New York: Simon and Schuster, 1989, p. 409.

**74** "Who knows about the Kennedys?" Kutler, op.cit., p. 29.

**75** "I hope it was because he was tired ..." Safire, William. *Before the Fall: An Inside View of the Pre-Watergate White House,* Garden City, N.Y.: Doubleday & Company, 1975, p. 210.

**78** "Do what the law requires. . ." Ambrose, *Nixon,* Vol. II, p. 460.

**78** "Your handshake came. . ." Nixon, op.cit., p. 560.

**78** "Your book, *Six Crises,* is not a bad book.", ibid., p. 564.

**79** "I'll give you some." Eisenhower, Julie Nixon. *Pat Nixon: The Untold Story.* New York: Kensington Publishing Corp., 1986, p, 510.

## CHAPTER NINE
### *A Cancer Close to the Presidency*

**81** "Don't try to be cute or cover up..." Ambrose, *Nixon,* Vol. II, p. 576-577.

**82** "Good deal... Play it tough..." ibid., p. 568.

**83** "We have a cancer—within, close to the Presidency." *The Presidential Transcripts.* New York: Dell Publishing Co., Inc., 1974, p. 99.

**83** "There's going to be a continual blackmail operation..." ibid., p. 107.

**83** "How much money do you need?" ibid., p. 110.

**84** "That's when you brought the facts. . ." Dean, John W. III, *Blind Ambition: The White House Years.* New York: Simon and Schuster, 1976, p. 262.

**85** "...two of the finest public servants. . ." Ambrose, Stephen E. *Nixon: Ruin and Recovery, 1973-1990,* Vol III. New York: Simon and Schuster, p 135-136.

**85** "I am not going to allow anybody..." Kutler, op.cit., p. 401.

**85** "Believe me, I knew nothing about it..." ibid., p. 476.

**85** "... God does bring the hardest problems to the strongest men," ibid., p. 488-489.

**86** "I don't want all this God——ed hypocrisy," ibid., p. 561.

**88** "I was hoping you fellows. . ." ibid., p. 194. (From Sanders, Donald. "Watergate Reminiscences," *Journal of American History,* March 1989, p. 1232-33.)

**89** "...smacks of dictatorship." Drew, Elizabeth. *Washington Journal.* New York: Random House, 1975, p. 53.

**89** "Has President Nixon gone crazy?" Nixon, op.cit., p. 935.

**89** "I am not a crook." Ambrose, *Nixon,* Vol. III, p. 271.

**90** "If my mother ever heard me use words like that..." ibid., p. 329.

**92** "...Dick Nixon has lied to me for the very last time," ibid., p. 420.

**92** "Dear Daddy—I love you..." Eisenhower, op.cit., p. 647.

**92** "History will treat you more kindly ..." Ambrose, *Nixon,* Vol. III, p. 427.

**94** "Therefore, I shall resign ..." Ambrose, *Nixon,* Vol. III, p. 435.

**94** "Good-bye, Mr. President." ibid., p. 445.

**94** "Our long national nightmare is over." Eisenhower, op.cit., p. 657.

CHAPTER TEN
*The Elder Statesman*

**95** "He appeared to have aged and shrunken .." Ford, Gerald R. *A Time to Heal: The Autobiography of Gerald R. Ford.* New York: Harper & Row, 1979, p. 170.

**96** "...They took it all away from me." ibid., p. 171.

**96** "I was wrong .." *New York Times,* September 9, 1974.

**98** " ... whose shoulder does she lean on?" Eisenhower, op.cit., p. 695.

**98** "It was a small thing, the break-in, *New York Times,* April 11, 1988.

**99** "From these humble roots..." "Fanfare to an Uncommon Man," *Time,* May 9, 1994, p. 48-9.

**100** "Bob, please get me the names of the Jews ..." Kutler, op.cit., p. 31.

**100** "Somewhere I figure somebody hurt him badly." Ambrose, *Nixon,* Vol. III, p. 588. (from Thompson, Kenneth W. *The Nixon Presidency.* Vol. VI of *Portraits of American Presidents,* University Press of America, 1987.

**100** "What starts the process, really, are the laughs and snubs and slights you get when you are a kid..." Ambrose, *Nixon,* Vol. III, p. 586-587. (from Clawson, Kenneth. "A Loyalist's Memoir," *Washington Post,* August 9, 1979.)

# Index